# ORTHO'S All About

# Backyard Structures

Meredith® Books
Des Moines, Iowa

Ortho® Books
An imprint of Meredith® Books

*Ortho's All About Backyard Structures*
Editor: Larry Erickson
Art Director: Tom Wegner
Contributing Writer: Martin Miller
Copy Chief: Catherine Hamrick
Copy and Production Editor: Terri Fredrickson
Contributing Copy Editor: Steve Hallam
Contributing Proofreaders: Kathy Eastman,
    Margaret Smith, Julie Sunne
Indexer: Donald Glassman
Electronic Production Coordinator: Paula Forest
Editorial and Design Assistants: Kathleen Stevens,
    Karen Schirm
Contributing Editorial Assistants: Janet Anderson,
    Colleen Johnson, Mary Irene Swartz
Production Director: Douglas M. Johnston
Book Production Managers: Pam Kvitne,
    Marjorie J. Schenkelberg

**Additional Editorial Contributions from
    Art Rep Services**
Director: Chip Nadeau
Designer: lk Design
Photo Editor: Nancy South
Writer: Clayton Bennett
Illustrator: John Teisberg, Shawn Wallace

**Meredith® Books**
Editor in Chief: James D. Blume
Design Director: Matt Strelecki
Managing Editor: Gregory H. Kayko

Director, Sales & Marketing, Retail: Michael A. Peterson
Director, Sales & Marketing, Special Markets:
    Rita McMullen
Director, Sales & Marketing, Home & Garden Center
    Channel: Ray Wolf
Director, Operations: George A. Susral

Vice President, General Manager: Jamie L. Martin

**Meredith Publishing Group**
President, Publishing Group: Christopher M. Little
Vice President, Consumer Marketing & Development:
    Hal Oringer

**Meredith Corporation**
Chairman and Chief Executive Officer: William T. Kerr

Chairman of the Executive Committee: E.T. Meredith III

Photographers
(Photographers credited may retain copyright ©
    to the listed photographs.)
John Fulkner: 4 (BL), 4-5 (center)
Charles Mann: 12-13, 78-79
Jerry Swanson: 42

All of us at Ortho® Books are dedicated to providing you
with the information and ideas you need to enhance your
home and garden. We welcome your comments and
suggestions about this book. Write to us at:
    Meredith Corporation
    Ortho Books
    1716 Locust St.
    Des Moines, IA 50309–3023

If you would like more information on other Ortho
products, call 800-225-2883 or visit us at www.ortho.com

**Note to the Readers:** Due to differing conditions, tools,
and individual skills, Meredith Corporation assumes no
responsibility for any damages, injuries suffered, or losses
incurred as a result of following the information published
in this book. Before beginning any project, review the
instructions carefully, and if any doubts or questions remain,
consult local experts or authorities. Because codes and
regulations vary greatly, you always should check with
authorities to ensure that your project complies with all
applicable local codes and regulations. Always read and
observe all of the safety precautions provided by
manufacturers of any tools, equipment, or supplies,
and follow all accepted safety procedures.

# PLANNING & CONSTRUCTION 4

# SEVEN SHELTERING OVERHEADS 12

# HARDWORKING SHEDS 42

# GAZEBO BUILDER'S TRIO 78

Cedar shakes add rustic character to this shed, left, and make it appear as if it has grown naturally out of its surroundings. It's a well-planned unity of function and aesthetics; the size, materials, and location complement the maintenance requirements of the large wooded yard and garden.

This abstract weathered overhead, below, isn't designed to provide shade—it defines the edge of the deck with a dramatic flair and adds a focal point to what would otherwise be an uneventful surface. The owners haven't overlooked the need for shade, however. They included the umbrella and the shaded arbor in their initial plans.

High in the hills, this enclosed summer house, above, offers a stunning view of the surrounding countryside—and a respite from inclement weather. The cupola, with its extension of the main roof lines, enhances the impression that the structure is also a "lookout" tower.

# PLANNING & CONSTRUCTION

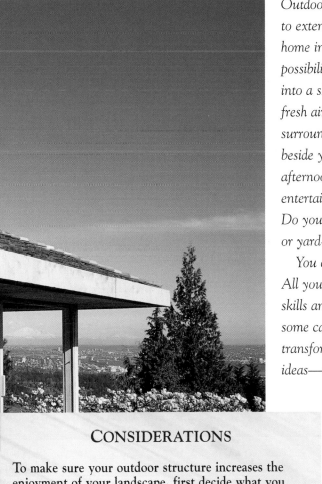

*Outdoor structures offer endless opportunities to extend the comfort and usefulness of your home into the landscape. Consider the possibilities. Do you want to turn your patio into a shaded oasis where you can savor the fresh air and the beauties of natural surroundings? How about a vine-covered arbor beside your garden for spending lazy afternoons, or a graceful gazebo for entertaining friends on summer evenings? Do you need storage space for gardening tools or yard-care supplies?*

*You can have any—or all—of these things. All you need is a goal, a detailed plan, modest skills and tools, a little time, and of course, some cash. Armed with information, you can transform your dreams—or just your good ideas—into reality.*

*That's where this book comes in. Inside, you'll find 16 complete plans and dozens of ideas to help you build projects that will enhance your outdoor living space. You'll build not only your pride of accomplishment, but also finished structures that you'll enjoy for many years to come.*

*Every successful project starts with a sound plan. This chapter will help you assess your needs, your building site, and your capabilities. It also reviews building basics you can use to create the structures and provides advice on selecting and buying materials.*

## CONSIDERATIONS

To make sure your outdoor structure increases the enjoyment of your landscape, first decide what you want to do—shade a patio, provide a stylish area for entertaining, or just store garden tools. Then make a wish list and a written plan from it. Create detailed drawings with measurements and shapes. If you alter the size of any of the structures in this book, use graph paper to record your modifications. Changes in even one dimension will affect other measurements in the plans. Here are some tips to get you started:

■ For shelter from the sun, a ventilated shade structure lets air flow through but blocks sunlight.
■ A solid roof keeps a deck or patio area dry during a rainstorm—a must in regions that get frequent rain.
■ Walls, fences, and shrubs help create a sense of enclosure, which makes an outdoor area feel private.
■ Large, open spaces lend themselves to parties and family gatherings—perfect for a shaded patio or gazebo.

# CONSTRUCTION PLANNING

*Here's a quick and easy way to see how your outdoor structure might look. Take a photograph of your house or the backyard location where you want to build. Have it printed large enough to see details clearly (an 8×10 is good). Get photocopies of the print so you can draw design ideas directly on the image. You'll save hours of effort as you experiment until you get just the design you want.*

Before you start building anything permanent in your yard, you'll have to do a little planning. You will need to choose a design for the structure, prepare a plan, establish a budget, and make a rough construction schedule. Proper planning will save you time and money in the long run and will help make the construction process frustration-free.

## THE RIGHT DESIGN

Your choice of design must be practical. For example, not only does a shade structure need to put shade on the patio at the right time of the day, the patio size itself needs to be suited to your needs. Small gatherings won't require much more space than the average dining room. For large parties, you may need more than twice that space. The same holds true for gazebos. And a storage shed should be large enough to contain all your tools and equipment.

Use rope to outline your structure on the ground. Move in furniture or equipment and adjust the rope until the size is adequate.

Your second design decision will be about aesthetics. Choosing materials, colors, and details that are used in your home will extend the style of your house into the landscape. That way, the structure will fit the overall look and feel of your property.

If you're building an unattached structure—a gazebo or garden shed, for example—your choice of materials and architectural style can be more flexible. You may want to use a design style that creates an unusual contrast with its surroundings or acts as a focal point.

## THE RIGHT SITE

**PURPOSE:** Where the structure goes will also be determined in part by its purpose. If you're adding shade to a new patio, you'll want easy access to the kitchen or family room. Storage sheds can be in the far corners of the property, but they should be close to the areas of their primary use. Gazebos will be somewhat removed from the house, but plan a pathway that coincides with the natural traffic flow.

**MOTHER NATURE:** Study the patterns of the sun and wind on your property; they will affect both location and construction, especially of overhead shade structures. You may want shade in the afternoon and sunlight

### MAPPING SHADE PATTERNS

The angle of the sun varies from one region to another and at different times of the year. Study shade patterns in your yard before building an overhead shade structure. These patterns and the angle of the sun will affect both the location and construction of your overhead.

## BUDGET AND WORK SCHEDULE

Before beginning work on any plan, estimate how much it will cost and how long it will take to complete.

### COSTS

Each of the plans in this book includes a materials list to help you figure costs. But you'll have to add costs for all the amenities you want to include—electrical wiring, new landscaping, and any other materials modifications you make. Make as detailed a shopping list as you can so suppliers can price your materials accurately and completely. That way, you won't run short in the middle of the project.

### TIME

Write down each step of the project and estimate the time it will take. Then add up your estimates. Or ballpark your total time with an old builder's gimmick: Simply divide the materials costs by the minimum wage. But even if you use this estimate, apply it to each step and make a construction calendar for yourself. A sequential plan will give you clear goals for each day's work.

If the result of all these computations indicates you will be giving up more weekends than you want to, consider hiring a professional for part of the job. Concrete work is a good project to contract.

Latticework is inexpensive and practical— it provides shade and lets in the gentle breezes.

This Victorian gazebo adds a stylish focal point to the landscape. It provides shade from the midday sun and shelter from the rain. Outdoor structures should account for local climate as well as family recreational needs.

in the morning and evening. Afternoon breezes may be welcome, but you may need to add a fence or plantings to suppress gusty winds. Mark the shade with stakes at various times of the day to get an idea of the sun's patterns across your yard.

### GETTING HELP

**SUPPLIERS:** Consult building-materials suppliers for prices and suggestions. You'll find that most will have a sincere interest in your plans as well as your materials list, and their suggestions may be all you need to get started (or to keep you going). Visit several and compare costs and quality.

**CONTRACTORS:** You may choose to contract part of the work, but don't jump at the first good bid. Get three bids and then weigh the benefits of contracting against your budget, time, and skills. A high price might make you feel much better about doing the job yourself. Some contractors even offer advice for a price, which may be all you need to stay on track.

## PLANS AND PERMITS

Check with your city or county building and zoning departments to find out whether your project will require a building permit and meets setback requirements. A freestanding structure may not require a permit, but most attached structures will.

If a permit is required, you will probably have to submit a site plan that shows the location of the proposed structure, along with more detailed drawings of items covered by codes—footings, foundations, and structure heights, for example. Most local codes set standards for the quality of materials, depths of footings, and sizes of posts and beams.

Building codes and zoning ordinances can affect your choice of materials as well as the size, type, position, and intended use of your new structure. Setbacks, for example, limit how close you can build to property lines. Get the facts early so you don't waste time planning a project that won't be approved.

If your proposal doesn't comply with the existing local zoning ordinances, you can apply for a variance—an exception—to the code requirements. A local board can grant a variance after holding a hearing for comments from neighbors.

# BUYING LUMBER

Building centers generally stock lumber in multiples of 2-foot lengths up to 20 feet long. Remember that most lumber is sold by nominal size rather than actual size. The chart *below* shows the difference.

## TYPES OF LUMBER

Lumber comes in a large variety of species and grades. Here's a quick primer to help you sort things out.

**DECAY-RESISTANT SPECIES:** Some species—redwood, cypress, and cedar—are naturally weather- and rot-resistant. Their beautiful color and weathering properties make them desirable for unfinished surfaces.

**PRESSURE-TREATED LUMBER:** Usually pine or fir, pressure-treated (PT) lumber is chemically treated to resist the elements. Buy lumber rated for ground contact for fence posts and shed foundation skids. Use above-grade stock for wall plates, framing members, and structural components within 6 inches of the soil.

**STRUCTURAL LUMBER:** Douglas fir and southern pine are the most common and are sold as either surfaced or rough-sawn. Use surfaced lumber for posts, beams, studs, and other framing members; use rough-sawn where you want a natural, textured look.

**FINISH LUMBER:** Use this for trim pieces.

Use decay-resistant woods for a natural, unfinished look that becomes more beautiful with exposure to the weather. If you paint the surfaces, any species of finish lumber will do.

**PLYWOOD:** Made from laminated veneers, plywood has great strength and stability and is ideal for floors, wall sheathing, and siding. Buy plywood rated for exterior use. It won't come apart in the rain.

The best lumber isn't always the best choice. For example, redwood and cedar are good options for a pavilion or gazebo that will be stained or left unfinished because these woods naturally resist decay and age beautifully. But a less expensive wood—Douglas fir, yellow southern pine, or western larch—is a better choice for a shed that you will paint.

## LINEAL AND BOARD FEET

When you shop for lumber, you may hear the terms "lineal foot" and "board foot." Small orders are often sold in *lineal feet*, which is the total length of a specific dimension of lumber required for the job. For example a dozen 8-foot 2×4s is 96 linear feet.

House-size orders are figured in *board feet*, a multiple of all the dimensions of the board.

Most modern building centers deal in unit prices. Just tell them specifically what you need; they'll print out an itemized price list before filling the order.

## READING GRADE STAMPS

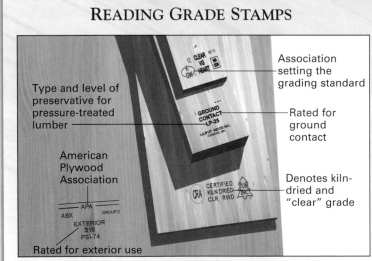

Type and level of preservative for pressure-treated lumber

American Plywood Association

Rated for exterior use

Association setting the grading standard

Rated for ground contact

Denotes kiln-dried and "clear" grade

Mills stamp lumber to identify its quality, moisture content, grade, and sometimes species. Standard lumber comes in various grades as either surfaced (smooth) or rough-sawn.

Plywood comes in four grades (A to D) and is designated for interior or exterior use. What you buy will depend on how exposed the wood surface will be, both to view and to weather.

## WHAT SIZE IS THAT REALLY?*

After it is cut, lumber is dried, planed, and smoothed, reducing its thickness and width. Nominal size, such as "1×4," refers to the size before drying and planing; actual size reflects the true, finished dimensions of the lumber.

| Nominal Size | Actual Size |
| --- | --- |
| 1×2 | ¾" × 1½" |
| 1×3 | ¾" × 2¼" |
| 1×4 | ¾" × 3½" |
| 1×6 | ¾" × 5½" |
| 1×8 | ¾" × 7¼" |
| 1×10 | ¾" × 9¼" |
| 1×12 | ¾" × 11¼" |
| 2×2 | 1½" × 1½" |
| 2×4 | 1½" × 3½" |
| 2×6 | 1½" × 5½" |
| 2×8 | 1½" × 7¼" |
| 2×10 | 1½" × 9¼" |
| 2×12 | 1½" × 11¼" |

*Sizes are for lumber surfaced dry. Lumber surfaced green will be slightly larger.*

## LUMBER GRADES

Lumber is graded by appearance and strength, with the grades set by lumber associations. Each has different rules, so a grade may mean different things in different places. Some chain stores even have their own grades.

**SMALL LUMBER:** Smaller pieces, such as 2×4s and 4×4s, have four grade levels.

■ **UTILITY GRADE** isn't strong enough for framing. Use it for blocking and partitions.

■ **STANDARD GRADE,** the most common, is suitable for light framing.

■ **CONSTRUCTION GRADE** is stronger and has fewer defects.

■ **STUD-GRADE** (for 2×4s), a quality usually between standard and construction grades, designates lumber specifically for use as studs.

**LARGE SIZES:** 2×6s and larger boards have three grades.

■ **NUMBER 2** is strong enough for most structural purposes, though it may have large knots and could be twisted or cracked.

■ **NUMBER 1,** with straighter grain and smaller knots than Number 2, is also better looking and stronger.

■ **STRUCTURAL** or **SELECT** boards are the strongest and are virtually free of knots.

**FINISH LUMBER:** Some associations use a letter system, with A being the best and D the poorest. Other associations use numbers:

■ **NUMBER 3** is suitable for rough use only.

■ **NUMBER 2** has plenty of knots.

■ **NUMBER 1** is nearly knot-free.

■ **CLEAR** lumber has no knots. It is expensive but well worth it for areas you want to show off.

Finish lumber is graded mainly by appearance, so the lumber number is less important than its looks. If you are painting your structure, save money by buying a cheaper grade and spend time filling holes and sanding. If you want a rustic look, you may prefer a lower grade.

## CONNECTORS

Metal connectors simplify the task of attaching any two framing members and they also strengthen the joint. They are made to fit standard lumber dimensions and accommodate fasteners, such as decking screws, lag screws, galvanized nails, and hex-head or carriage bolts. Building-supply centers stock many connectors, and they can special order less common items that are out of stock.

For safety and warranty protection, always follow the manufacturer's recommendations when installing framing connectors. The most common framing connectors are shown in the illustration, *right.*

## MAXIMUM RECOMMENDED SPANS

A beam can usually safely span a foot for each inch of depth: So a 4×6 will span 6 feet, a 4×8 will span 8 feet, and so on. Posts should be set 6 to 10 feet apart, and spans greater than 12 feet should be avoided.

| Beam Size | Spacing Between Members | | |
|---|---|---|---|
| | 4' | 8' | 12' |
| 2×6 | 7' 11" | 7' 0" | 6' 3" |
| 2×8 | 10' 6" | 9' 6" | 8' 0" |
| 2×10 | 13' 4" | 12' 0" | 10' 6" |
| 2×12 | 16' 3" | 14' 6" | 12' 9" |
| 4×4 | 6' 11" | 6' 0" | 5' 3" |
| 4×6 | 10' 10" | 9' 6" | 8' 3" |
| 4×8 | 14' 4" | 12' 6" | 11' 0" |
| 4×10 | 18' 3" | 16' 0" | 14' 0" |
| 4×12 | 22' 2" | 19' 6" | 17' 0" |
| 6×6 | 14' 2" | 11' 3" | 9' 6" |
| 6×10 | 19' 8" | 17' 1" | 15' 3" |

## HOW MANY NAILS PER POUND? (NUMBERS ARE APPROXIMATE)

| Penny | Length | Common | Finish |
|---|---|---|---|
| 2d | 1" | 870 | 1,350 |
| 3d | 1¼" | 543 | 850 |
| 4d | 1½" | 290 | 600 |
| 5d | 1¾" | 254 | 300 |
| 6d | 2" | 236 | 200 |
| 7d | 2¼" | 223 | 125 |
| 8d | 2½" | 135 | |
| 10d | 3" | 92 | |
| 12d | 3½" | 61 | |
| 16d | 3¾" | 47 | |
| 20d | 4" | 29 | |

**FRAMING CONNECTORS**

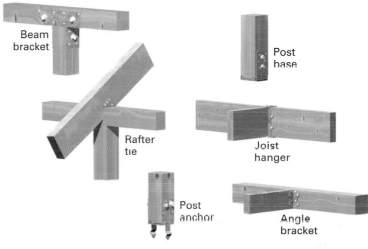

Beam bracket

Post base

Rafter tie

Joist hanger

Post anchor

Angle bracket

# FOOTINGS & FOUNDATIONS

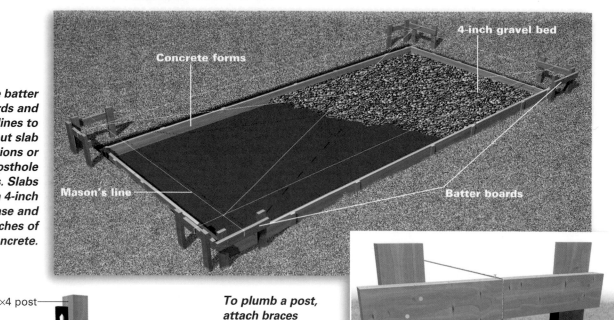

*Use batter boards and mason's lines to lay out slab foundations or posthole footings. Slabs require a 4-inch gravel base and 4 inches of poured concrete.*

Concrete forms

4-inch gravel bed

Mason's line

Batter boards

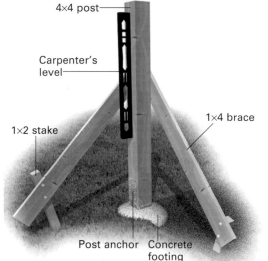

4×4 post

Carpenter's level

1×2 stake

1×4 brace

Post anchor   Concrete footing

*To plumb a post, attach braces between the post and ground. Adjust them until the post is plumb on two adjacent sides. Then fasten the post securely in the post anchor (or for posts below grade, pour concrete in the hole).*

*Batter boards take the guesswork out of site layout. Make them from scrap 2×4s with the crosspiece nailed 3 to 4 inches below the top. Point the "legs" so they're easy to drive into the ground.*

The plans in this book require careful layout, and most call for a foundation—either post footings or a concrete slab.

## SITE PREPARATION

Mark corners with temporary stakes. Then use batter boards (pointed 2-foot 2×4 legs with an 18-inch crosspiece) and mason's lines to mark the perimeter of your slab or post locations.

Drive the batter boards at right angles to each other (about 18 inches beyond the corners), as shown in the illustration, *above*. Tie mason's lines to the crosspieces and run them between the batter boards. Adjust the lines until the diagonals are the same length (that will square the corners). Drop a plumb bob at the intersections of the lines and stake those points to mark corner post centers or excavation and slab corners. Then measure

and stake remaining post centers. If you're laying a slab, line the ground from one stake to another with powdered chalk or spray paint. That's the line along which you'll dig.

Excavate the area (or postholes) to the proper depth (8 inches for a concrete slab, 3 to 4 feet for posts) and build forms for concrete (if you're building a slab or poured piers). If your project requires a permit, make sure an inspector checks it before you pour any concrete. Even if you don't need a permit, build strong forms (2× stock, staked with 2×4s every 2 to 3 feet). Shoring up a sagging form filled with concrete is nearly impossible.

## REINFORCEMENTS

Slabs need to be strengthened with reinforcing wire, and those with a continuous perimeter footing call for steel bars, or rebar.

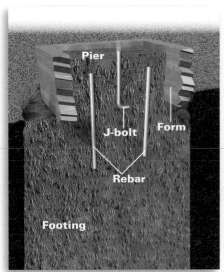

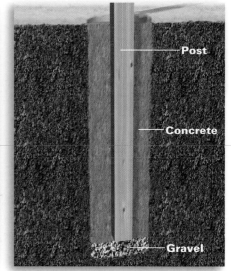

*You can form and pour footings and piers together (placing post anchors before concrete sets up) or set ready-* *made piers in place before poured footings set up. If local building codes allow, set pressure-treated* *posts directly into holes with gravel at the bottom. Then fill the holes with concrete.*

Cut rebar with a hacksaw or a circular saw with a metal-cutting blade (wear safety glasses) and set it in the footings parallel to the forms.

## MIX BY HAND OR TRUCK IT?

A cubic yard—the unit of measure for concrete—equals 27 cubic feet: enough to form a 6×9-foot slab 6 inches thick. For small tasks like pouring a couple of footings, buy premixed bags. For a quarter-cubic-yard or less, mixing your own from dry ingredients might not be too difficult. Loads of one yard or more are better ordered for delivery in a mixer truck.

**PREMIX:** Premix bags contain everything but the water, it's easy to mix. A 60-pound sack makes about half a cubic foot ($\frac{1}{52}$ of a yard). Dump the mix in one end of a wheelbarrow. Add water at the edge of the dry mix and pull the mix in a little at a time.

**DRY MIX:** Mixing your own dry ingredients is not easy, but if you're ready to do the work, use a heavy-duty wheelbarrow to mix materials near the site, or rent a power mixer that you can roll right to the site. In either case, mix 1 part portland cement, 2 parts sand and 3 parts sand. Put the gravel in first. Then add sand, cement, and water.

**1.** Blend dry ingredients. If using a wheelbarrow, push the mixture to the back.

**2.** Add water a little at a time. In a wheelbarrow, rake some of the dry mix into the water with a hoe.

**3.** Continue to blend water gradually, until the mix resembles a thick milkshake.

**READY-MIX:** If you need a mixer truck, ask the company how close they can get to the

building site. A truck equipped with a concrete pumper is much more versatile than one that hauls concrete. Concrete takes less than four hours to set, depending on weather conditions. So make sure all is ready before the concrete truck arrives.

## FILL 'EM UP

Fill the forms with concrete and level it by drawing a straight 2×4 over the forms with a sawing motion. Insert any post anchors or other fasteners while the concrete is wet.

Smooth the surface with a wood or metal float, working quickly with a light touch. Let the concrete cure for three days to a week.

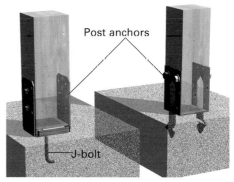

*Post anchors can be set directly in wet concrete, or fastened to a J-bolt. Both methods work equally well, and will anchor your posts securely.*

## FINISHING TOUCH

As soon as you pour the concrete, draw a screed board across the surface to level it. Finish large surfaces with a bull float. Use a light touch; gouges in fresh concrete can be difficult to fix. To smooth out areas you can reach, use a wood float, followed by a metal trowel.

# SEVEN SHELTERING OVERHEADS

*You can attach an overhead to an existing structure or build it to stand alone. Either design will provide an oasis of shade, shelter, or decoration. Most overheads are built over patios or decks and enhance not only their beauty but also their comfort.*

*An overhead can transform your landscape. It subtly contains you in a direction—up—that provides cozy comfort with a boundary that is sometimes only suggested by an open framework or frail lattice. Overheads put a ceiling on your outdoor room.*

*If you are not certain of the design you want, the best starting point for your project is in someone else's yard. Visit friends who have covered patios to get a sense of what you find most comfortable. You'll probably respond differently to variations in height, color, and material. Learning from the experience of others is much less expensive than trial-and-error lessons at home.*

*By definition, an overhead has a high profile. Patios may hide behind hedges, but overheads stand fully exposed to the strain of high winds and the other elements. It's important to build your overhead with style, and also strong enough to withstand its environment.*

*This chapter offers help on both fronts. You'll learn principles of design and construction that you can apply to your specific project.*

*The plans presented here can be built as described or modified to fit your requirements. Each plan includes illustrations, step-by-step instructions, a materials list, and tips to make your job easier.*

## ADAPTING PLANS TO SUIT YOUR NEEDS

As you study these plans, you may decide you want to adapt them to your site. That should not be a problem. The plans share many building techniques and design elements. Imagine how you might fit part of one plan with another. For examples of the creative possibilities, we've altered a few of our own plans, providing variations on pages 38–41.

*An overhead structure serves a valuable purpose by defining an outdoor living area without placing a solid roof over your head. An open design like this one creates a sense of enclosure for your deck or patio. Unless you often need complete shelter from unrelenting sunlight or frequent rain, an open overhead structure—one that lets air and light flow through—provides a comfortable and inviting outdoor room for you and your guests.*

## FROST PROTECTION

In cold climates, codes require footings to be set below the frost line to prevent structures from heaving when the ground freezes. Check with your local building inspector to make sure the footing holes meet code requirements. The inspector must check the holes before you pour the concrete.

# ATTACHED SHADE STRUCTURE

*This slat-covered canopy, supported on decorative beams, provides shade and airy ventilation for a patio. The structure can be readily adapted to support a solid roof.*

Even a simple canopy can be elegant. Decorative cuts on the ends of the beam and crossbeams—plus trim-faced posts—give this design a well-crafted look.

## LEDGER

To meet most building codes, you'll need to leave at least 6½ feet of headroom under the outer beam. Mark the location of the ledger so that its lower edge is at least 7 feet, 2 inches above the highest post base.

Cut away the siding so you can attach the ledger directly to the house. Set your circular saw to the depth of the siding—just to the sheathing. Next, find the wall studs: Look for nails in the siding or sheathing or use an electronic stud finder. Cut the ledger to size, hold it in place so you can see the stud locations, and mark it at the stud lines.

Next, slip metal Z flashing under the siding to prevent moisture from building up under the ledger.

Slip the ledger under the outer edge of the flashing and tack it in place with nails; drill holes at the stud marks for ½-inch lag screws, and recess them for washers. Put washers under the heads of 5-inch lag screws and drive them with a socket wrench.

On a brick house, there's nothing to cut. Drill holes for masonry anchors. Attach the ledger in the anchors with lag screws.

## POST FOOTINGS

This plan uses posts spaced 8 feet on center, but you can increase the span if you use larger posts and a heavier beam. See *page 9* for recommended post spacing and beam spans.

Lay out the site with batter boards and mason's lines (*see page 10*) and mark the posthole locations. Each post should be set so it will lie directly below a crossbeam, so check your measurements.

Dig footing holes to specifications required by local building codes. After the footing holes are approved by a building inspector, fill them with concrete.

While the concrete is still wet, place a pier block, a post anchor, or a J-bolt in each footing. This is when you should make sure your posts are centered under a crossbeam; the footings can be a little off center after you've poured the concrete, but you can

**PLAN VIEW**

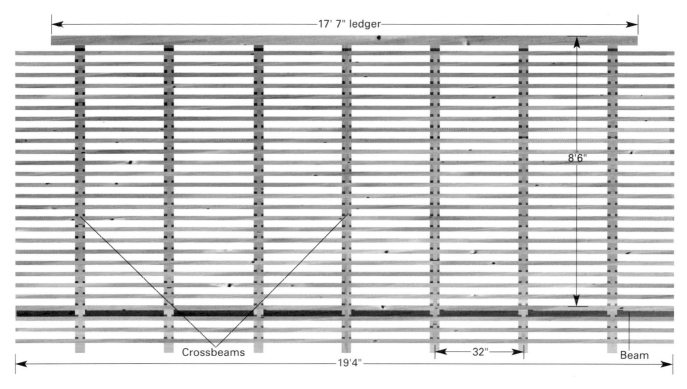

17' 7" ledger

8'6"

Crossbeams

32"

Beam

19'4"

*Placed at equal intervals, slats laid on edge provide a good balance between shade and design.*

locate the anchors precisely in the wet concrete. Measure your post locations again and set the anchors precisely. For protection against moisture damage, the anchors or piers should hold the bottom of each post at least 1 inch off the ground. Let the concrete cure for three days to a week.

## POSTS

Set uncut 4×4 posts on their piers or anchors. Make braces from scrap 1×4 lumber (*staked on one end as shown in the illustration, page 10*), and tack them to the posts on two adjacent sides. Plumb the posts on two sides with a carpenter's level, then drive the stakes into the ground. Use a line level or a carpenter's level on a straight 2×4 to mark each post at a point that is level with the bottom of the ledger. This mark represents the top of the 4×8 main beam. Measure down to the depth of the beam (about 7¼ inches for a 4×8) and mark a cut line.

Take the posts down and cut them to length. Treat the cut ends with preservative sealer. Nail post caps to the tops of the posts and put the posts back up, plumbing with the braces. Fasten them to the piers or post anchors. Leave the braces in place.

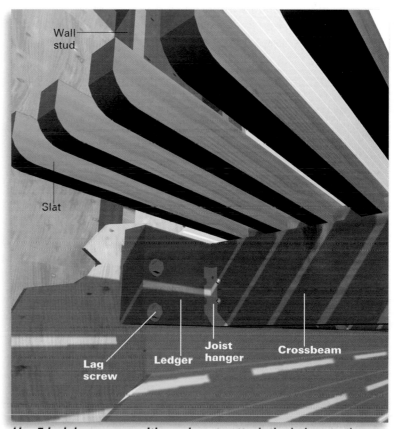

Wall stud

Slat

Lag screw

Ledger

Joist hanger

Crossbeam

*Use 5-inch lag screws with washers to attach the ledger to the studs. Attach crossbeams to the ledger with joist hangers.*

# ATTACHED SHADE STRUCTURE
*continued*

*Finished ends add a decorative touch to overhead beams. The pattern you choose will become one of the elements that defines the style of your structure. Look for a pleasing shape to adapt from your house or landscape so your overhead structure will complement its surroundings.*

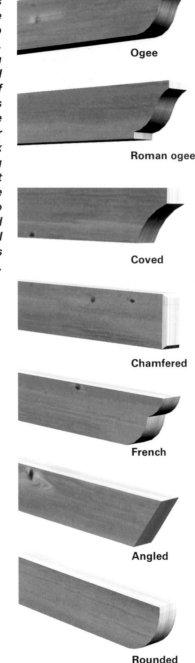

Ogee

Roman ogee

Coved

Chamfered

French

Angled

Rounded

## MAIN BEAM

Cut the beam to length and make any decorative cuts in its ends before installing it. Lift the beam into place and set it in the post caps. Measure the ends to make sure they extend equally beyond the end posts. Fasten the beam securely in the post caps.

If your site requires two beams for one span, center the joint on a post. Attach the ends to each other and to the post with a T-strap.

## DECORATIVE CROSS BEAMS

If you plan to finish the crossbeams with decorative cuts, make the cuts before installing them.

To cut duplicate patterns, draw your design on a thin sheet of plywood or a stiff piece of cardboard. Cut the cardboard or plywood to create a tracing template, and mark the pattern on the crossbeams. Cut straight lines with a circular saw, curved lines with a jigsaw. Use a router and bit with a guide bearing to create rounded or chamfered ends.

## INSTALLING CROSS BEAMS

Mark the ledger 9½ inches from each end and at 32-inch intervals for joist hangers. Where crossbeams sit above a post, they should be centered (you can fudge a bit to make sure). Nail the joist hangers centered on the marks. Cut the crossbeams to length and nail them to the joist hangers. Toenail the outer ends to the beam with 16d nails.

## CANOPY

To keep canopy slats from warping, cut blocks from 2×2 stock to fit between the slats. Each block should be about 2½ inches long. Using a radial arm saw, cut several blocks at once; a large canopy may need hundreds of blocks. Predrill the blocks and fasten them and the canopy with 20d nails.

## POST TRIM

Now you can remove the temporary bracing and install the 2×4 trim to the post faces. Cut the trim to length (the front and back pieces will extend to the top of the main beam, the side pieces to the bottom of the beam). Mark and cut shallow recesses in the pieces that cover the post anchor so the trim fits snugly over the bolts and anchors. Using two 16d nails every 24 inches, attach all four 2×4s to each post.

## SUN AND SHADE

Because the space between each 2×3 slat is the same as the depth of the slat (2 inches), a slatted canopy will provide full shade during the hottest part of the day if the slats run from east to west. For more sun below the trellis, increase the spacing or use smaller slats.

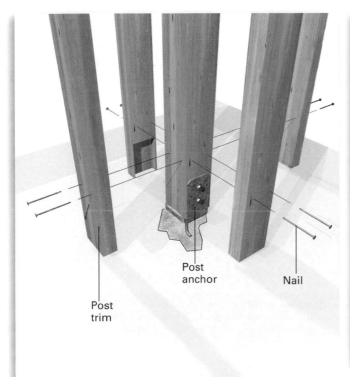

Cover the post anchors, and give the posts a finished look by nailing 2×4s to all four sides of each post. Recess the 2×4s where they fit over the anchor and bolts.

To nail slats at equal intervals, place 2×2 spacers between the slats as you fasten them. To correct bent or bowed boards, line up each slat over its full length before nailing. Predrill the spacers and use 20d galvanized nails to secure the slats and blocks to the cross beams.

## CANOPY WORKING TIPS

**SPEED:** Reduce repetitive cutting tasks with a fence stop on a power miter saw or table saw.

**ORDER:** Work your way from the outer edge until you are within a few feet of the house. Then measure precisely to the ledger; if the last slat is not parallel, cut the blocks to gradually make up the remaining distance.

## LAYING A PATIO SURFACE

A weatherproof patio surface is the perfect complement to any overhead. Pavers and bricks can easily be laid on a bed of compacted sand. Here's how:

Mark off the area for the patio and excavate to a depth of 8 inches. Set bricks on end for edging around the perimeter. Lay landscape fabric over the excavated area. Spread 4 inches of gravel and 2 inches of sand, then level and tamp it firmly. Place pavers, brick, or stone (such as flagstone, slate, or granite) on the sand. Level the surface, and sweep sand into the joints.

## MATERIALS FOR ATTACHED SHADE STRUCTURE

| Description | Material/Size | Quantity |
|---|---|---|
| Ledger | 2×6 lumber, 18' | 1 |
| Lag screws and washers | Coated or stainless, 5" | 26 |
| Footings | Poured concrete, 4–5 cu. ft.* | 3 |
| Piers (if used) | Poured or ready-made | 3 |
| Post anchors | 4×4 | 3 |
| Bolts or screws | For post anchors | 6 |
| Posts | 4×4 lumber, 10' | 3 |
| Post trim | 2×4 lumber, 12' | 12 |
| Beam brackets | To hold 4×8 beam | 3 |
| Bolts | For beam brackets | 6 |
| Beam | 4×8 lumber, 20' | 1 |
| Joist hangers | To hold 4×6 cross beams | 7 |
| Crossbeams | 4×6 lumber, 12' | 7 |
| Slats | 2×3 lumber | 600 lin. ft. |
| Spacer blocks | 2×2 lumber | 50 lin. ft. |
| Nails | 16d and 20d HDG | 2 lbs. each |

*Average amount; will vary by site

# AWNING OPTION

This variation of the previous plan features a pitched awning roof. Structurally, it differs in two important ways: how the ledger is attached to the house and how the canopy is installed and covered. Instructions for building these and some other differences are provided in this section.

## LEDGER

Locate the ledger high enough so the pitch of the roof will place the bottom of the front beam 6½ feet from the ground.

You can experiment—with a helper—using scrap 2×6 "ledger" and a "dummy" rafter. Adjust the height of your scrap ledger until the bottom of the rafter is 85¼ inches above the ground. That will account for the height of the beam.

*Without an overhead to provide protection from the sun, this patio would be uncomfortably bright and hot. An awning keeps the patio shaded in the early afternoon, making it a pleasant, usable outdoor space. Exposed roof sheathing and Y-braces contribute a casual look.*

4×4 Y-braces    Roof sheathing

Follow the directions on *page 14* for marking the ledger position, adding 3½ inches to the height of the cutout to accommodate the backing strip. Pry back the edge of the siding above the cutout just far enough to slip Z flashing underneath. Measure and cut a 1×4 backing strip the same length as the cutout, and slide the backing strip under the outer edge of the flashing. Fasten the backing strip, nailing it to the studs. Attach the ledger to the house immediately underneath the backing strip and install joist hangers on the ledger at 16-inch intervals, starting 9½ inches from one end.

## POSTS AND BEAM

Lay out and set the posts on 8-foot centers as shown on *pages 10 and 14*, setting them on footings and piers and bracing them with 1×4s. Measure and cut the posts (8'8" in this design) and leave the braces in place. Then install the beam as described on *page 16*. Miter cut 21-inch lengths (along the longest edge) of 4×4 for the post braces and attach them to the posts with 20d nails.

## RAFTERS AND SHEATHING

The exact rafter angle will vary from site to site, so you will have to determine it after the beam is installed.

Start by laying a rafter on the beam and bring its ledger end (bottom edge) even with the bottom of the ledger. Measure the space from the top of the rafter to the top of the ledger. Take the rafter down and mark that measurement on its top edge. Cut the rafter from that point to the lower corner. Turn the rafter over and cut the same angle where it rests on the beam. Use this rafter as a template to mark the others. Install the end rafters first, then the remaining rafters.

Cover the rafters with ½- or ⅝-inch exterior-grade plywood. Start flush at the outside edges of the crossbeams, making sure that the interior sheathing edges are centered on a rafter. Or, you can center the sheathing on a rafter first and cut off excess at the end of the roof. Fasten the sheathing with 8d nails, staggering the joints.

## ROOF

Finish the structure with roll roofing, wood, or composition shingles if your local fire code allows you to use them. Use a double layer of 30-pound felt under the shingles to waterproof the structure. When the roof is covered, slide a length of L flashing under the Z flashing and fasten it with 4d hot-dipped galvanized nails.

**PLAN VIEW**

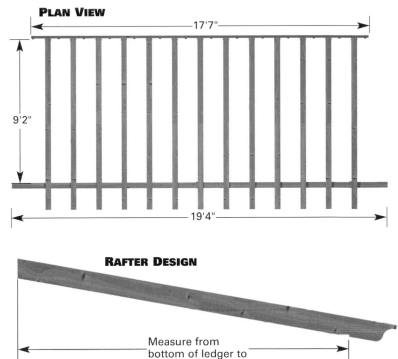

17'7"

9'2"

19'4"

**RAFTER DESIGN**

Measure from bottom of ledger to front edge of beam

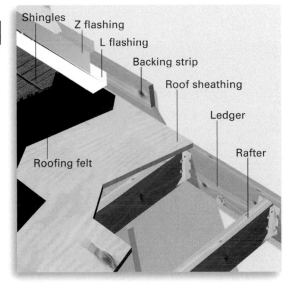

Shingles

Z flashing

L flashing

Backing strip

Roof sheathing

Ledger

Rafter

Roofing felt

*The Z and L flashing work together to direct rain down the roof instead of behind the ledger.*

## MATERIALS ADDITIONS FOR AWNING OPTION

| Description | Material/Size | Quantity |
|---|---|---|
| Joists (and hangers) | 2×6 lumber, 10' | 13 |
| Backing strip | 1×4 lumber, 18" | 1 |
| Flashing | Sheet aluminum, 12" roll | 20 lin. ft. |
| Post bracing | 4×4 lumber, 12' | 1 |
| Sheathing | ½" or ⅝" exterior plywood | 7 |
| Roofing | Roofing felt | 220 sq. ft. |
| | Composition shingles | 220 sq. ft. |

# LOW-PROFILE, ATTACHED OVERHEAD

*The posts for this overhead structure can be attached to a deck, fastened to post anchors set in concrete footings, or fastened to an existing slab. Lattice panels and rails provide a subtle balance of shade, enclosure, and cool breezes.*

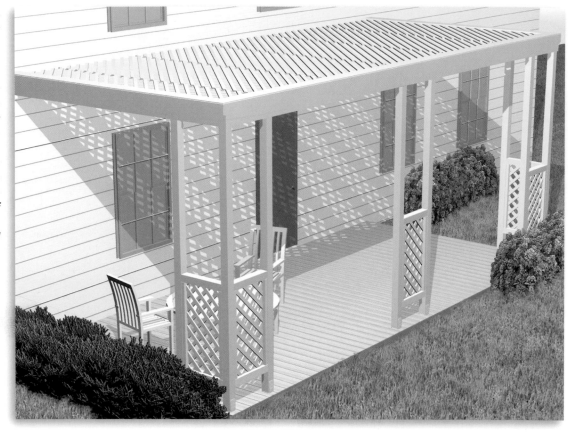

A high overhead structure is impractical for some homeowners because it won't fit in the space between the first and second floors or below the roof line. This low-profile design solves that problem.

## MINIMUM MEASUREMENTS

To meet building code requirements in most locations, you will need at least a foot of unobstructed wall space above a door or window to attach the ledger board. Measure carefully before you set the final height of the supporting posts.

If you have a low roof overhang, you'll also need to make sure the joists will clear the bottom of the overhang. Mark the wall a couple of inches over a window or door (that's where the bottom edge of the ledger will go), then make another mark 7½ inches above the first to locate the the top of the ledger. Run a level board out from the top mark past the edge of the overhang.

If your level is below the overhang, you're ready to begin. If not, you may be able to trim the rafter tails or fascia without disturbing the roof sheathing or the roofing itself.

This design easily adapts to sites that have different dimensions; but if you change the dimensions to fit your site, try to keep the overall size in increments of 2 feet.

## LEDGER

Locate the ledger so that the bottom edge will be at least 2 inches above any doors or windows. Then measure and mark a point 3½ inches from each end of the ledger to leave space for the 4×8 beams.

Cut and bolt the ledger to the wall (*see page 14*). If the ledger will not be protected by the roof overhang, insert Z flashing to keep moisture from collecting behind it.

## LAYOUT

Lay out the site (using the outer perimeter of the beams as your dimensions) with batter boards and mason's lines (*see pages 10 and 14*), and mark footing locations accurately. Corner post faces are 2½ inches inside the mason's lines. The posts adjacent to the corners are 24 inches on center; the middle pair is 19 inches on center. Dig the footings, pour them, and install J–bolts or piers. Let the concrete cure for three days to a week.

**FRAMING PLAN**

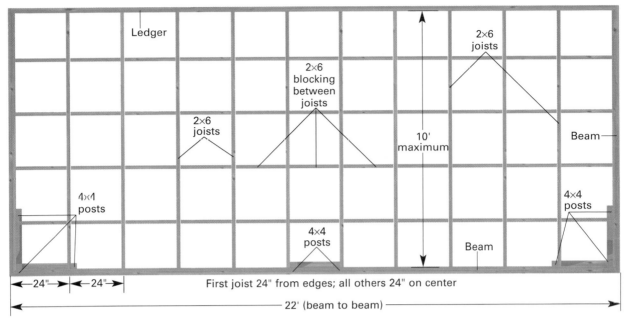

Ledger

2×6 joists

2×6 blocking between joists

2×6 joists

2×6 joists

Beam

10' maximum

4×4 posts

4×4 posts

4×4 posts

Beam

24"  24"  First joist 24" from edges; all others 24" on center

22' (beam to beam)

If you're building on an existing slab, local codes may allow you to install anchors directly on it, if it's at least 4 inches thick. If you're building a new deck, use precast piers and fasten the deck beams to the posts.

## POSTS AND BEAMS

Set the corner posts in post anchors and brace them plumb. Mark them at level with the top of the ledger, using a carpenter's level on a straight 2×4, or a water level.

Cut one corner post at the mark and notch it on two sides for the 4×8 beams. (Make a series of 1-inch cuts about ¼ inch apart, knock out the waste with a hammer, and smooth the notch with a chisel). Cut and notch the other corner post, brace both posts plumb, and nail them to the anchors. Mark the heights of the remaining posts (run a line from corner posts to mark them). Cut and install the remaining posts, notching them on the side that faces out.

Measure the beams, allowing for mitered corners. Then cut and install them with coated or stainless lag screws or carriage bolts.

Recess the holes for washers. Use angle brackets to attach the beams to the ledger.

## JOISTS AND BLOCKING

Mark the ledger and front beam at 24-inch intervals. Nail joist hangers at the marks. Fit the joists and nail them to the hangers.

Snap chalk lines across the tops of the joists on 24-inch centers for the blocking. Cut the blocks to length and nail the top edges flush with the top of the beams.

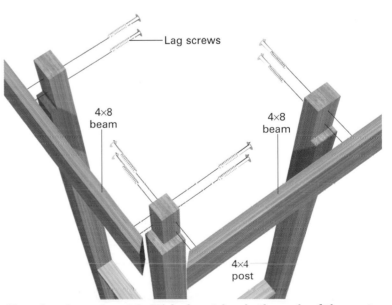

Lag screws

4×8 beam

4×8 beam

4×4 post

*Use a hand saw to cut 1×7¼-inch notches in the ends of the posts. This provides a surface for the beams to rest on. Miter or butt-joint the beam ends at the corners. Fasten the beams to the posts with lag screws or carriage bolts.*

## WORKING ON TOP OF LATTICE

To work from above and not break through the lattice, use two 2-foot plywood squares. Kneel on one and place the other on the next square. Reposition the platforms as you move.

# LOW-PROFILE, ATTACHED OVERHEAD
*continued*

## LATTICE PANELS

Paint or stain the lattice panels, or buy them prepainted. Use full sheets wherever possible, making cuts so lattice ends are centered on a joist or block. If you need to cut a panel to fit, avoid running the saw over the staples holding the slats together. The saw will cut the staples, but the blade will wear out much sooner. Fasten the panels with 4d HDG nails.

*Place 4×8-foot lattice panels on top of the joists and blocking. Center the panel edges on joists, blocking, and beams. Fasten the lattice with HDG 4d box nails. Nail 2×2-inch trim in 2-foot squares on top of the lattice.*

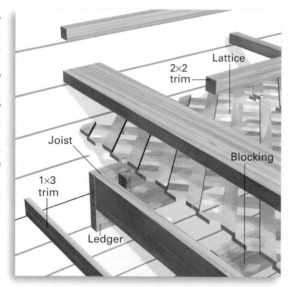

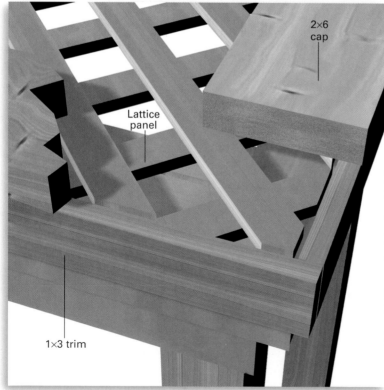

With the lattice panels in place, fasten pieces of 1×3 trim to the outside edges of the beams, flush with the top surface of the lattice. The trim will help support 2×6 caps laid flat on the beams.

## CANOPY TRIM

Set the inner edge of the 2×6 cap so it is flush with the inside edge of each beam. With the 2×6 cap in place, install 2×2 trim over the joists and blocking to help secure the lattice panels.

Complete the canopy by nailing 1×3 trim under the overhanging cap. The trim hides the lattice edge and also serves as a molding.

## RAILING PANELS

To make the decorative panels at the base of the posts, cut 2×4 rails (at any height that looks right to you) and toenail them to the posts. Make frames of 1×1 stops and install one of them on one side of the opening. Cut lattice and secure it with the second frame.

## FREESTANDING ALTERNATIVE

If you don't have room to clear the roof overhang and you can't trim it without disturbing the roof, consider adapting this plan as a freestanding (detached) overhead a few feet from the house. You will need to add rear posts and another beam to take the place of the ledger attached to the house.

To make lattice inserts, cut 2×4 rails to fit between the posts, and toenail them in place. Measure the openings and cut lattice panels and 1×1 frames to fit. Install one frame, insert a lattice panel, and then install the other frame. Make sure the panel assemblies are centered on the rails and posts.

# FINISHES AND MAINTENANCE

Painted

Stained

Weathered

**PAINTING:** Choose a good quality outdoor paint (latex is much easier to use than synthetic alkyd resin paints) and apply an undercoat or primer. Always read and follow directions. Manufactured lattice often comes with an undercoat already applied. If you construct lattice yourself, paint the pieces before you assemble them, then touch up as needed after the lattice is installed.

Paint not only beautifies but also keeps moisture from reaching and rotting the wood surface. Good paint may last 10 years. Check painted surfaces on an annual basis; when it's evident that the paint is no longer doing its job, avoid the urge to wait for one more year—it's easier and cheaper to repaint promptly than to replace rotted wood after it has been neglected.

**STAINING:** Stains penetrate wood instead of covering it. Semitransparent stains tint the surface but do not hide the wood's natural grain; if you want to mask lower grades of lumber or want a covering with more pigment, choose a solid-color stain.

Rough or saw-textured lumber is a better candidate to stain than paint, but all stained lumber may need periodic restaining to counter the effects of weathering. The wood will last longer if you treat it with a clear water repellent after staining it. Follow the recommendations provided by the stain manufacturer.

**WEATHERING:** Woods with a natural resistance to decay—such as redwood, cedar, and cypress—weather beautifully and can be left in their natural state or treated only with a clear water repellent or other protective finish. These woods are more expensive than common structural woods, such as fir, pine, or larch. Remember that weathered wood may have more splinters than boards covered with paint or other types of finish. Finally, consider how the structure will look after the wood has aged: If it will seem out of place next to a neatly painted house, then consider painting the wood instead.

## MATERIALS FOR LOW-PROFILE, ATTACHED OVERHEAD

| Description | Material/Size | Quantity |
|---|---|---|
| Ledger | 2×8 lumber, 12' | 2 |
| Footings (if used) | Poured concrete, 4–5 cu. ft.* | 3 |
| Posts | 4×4 lumber, 8' minimum | 8 |
| Perimeter beams | 4×8 lumber, 12' | 4 |
| Joists | 2×6 lumber, 10' | 10 |
| Blocking | 2×6 lumber | 88 lin. ft. |
| Lattice | 4×8 sheets wood or vinyl lattice | 8 |
| Trim | 2×6 lumber, 12' | 4 |
| | 2×2 lumber | 190 lin. ft. |
| | 1×3 lumber, 12' | 4 |
| | 2×4 lumber, 16' | 1 |
| | 1×1 lumber | 80-90 lin. ft. |
| Lag screws and washers | Coated or stainless, ½"×5" | 32 |
| Post anchors | To hold 4×4 posts | 8 |
| Bolts for post anchors | As required; usually 2 each | 16 |
| Beam brackets | To hold 4×8 beam | 8 |
| Bolts for beam brackets | As required, usually 2 each | 16 |
| Joist hangers | To hold 2×6 joists and blocking | 108 |
| Angle brackets | To attach end beams to ledger | 6 |
| Nails for joist hangers | 1½" hanger nails | 2 lbs. |
| Nails for 2×6 lumber | 16d HDG | 5 lbs. |
| Nails for light trim | 8d HDG | 1 lb. |
| Nails for lattice panels | 4d HDG | 2 lbs. |

*Average amount; will vary by site

# FREESTANDING OVERHEAD

*This freestanding overhead— a low-pitched roof supported by posts— provides shelter for outdoor dining and socializing, with plenty of space for a picnic table and a grill.*

In regions where rain often spoils picnics, parties, and other activities, a simple roof overhead will reclaim the outdoors. This structure provides enough room for a picnic table, outdoor chairs, or benches for family relaxation. A freestanding overhead with a solid roof is also useful in dry climates, offering protection from the heat and glare of the midday sun.

This structure is easier to build if you pour the footings first and add the surface later. The surface can be anything from poured concrete to bark chips.

## STRUCTURE

This shelter consists of a gable roof canopy on a framework of 4×4 beams and 2×6 cross ties. The beams and cross ties are supported by 4×4 posts set on concrete footings. Post anchors hold it firmly in place.

You won't need diagonal post bracing unless the posts are especially tall, or your area has frequent or severe high winds.

## FOOTINGS

Use batter boards and mason's lines (*see page 10*) to establish the centers for the corner footings, and stake all footing locations.

Using a hand posthole digger or a power auger, dig the footing holes (at least a foot wide) to the depth required by your local building code. Place 6 inches of gravel in each hole, then fill with concrete. Center a post anchor in the concrete while it's wet. Most building codes call for post anchors that hold wood posts at least an inch above the ground. Before the concrete sets, check the post anchors to make sure they are level with each other and are at the required height.

## POSTS

When the footings have cured (three days to a week), set the corner posts in the post anchors. Brace each post plumb and— depending on the configuration of the anchor—fasten them to the anchors with bolts or screws. When all the corner posts are plumb, mark one at the height of the beam (80 inches in this design, although your posts can be somewhat higher if you wish) and— using a line level or water level—mark the remaining corner posts. Cut them at your mark. (Tip: Tape heavy paper around the post to make an even cut line). Install the remaining posts, bracing them for plumb. Use a line strung between corner posts to mark and cut them.

**FRAMING PLAN**

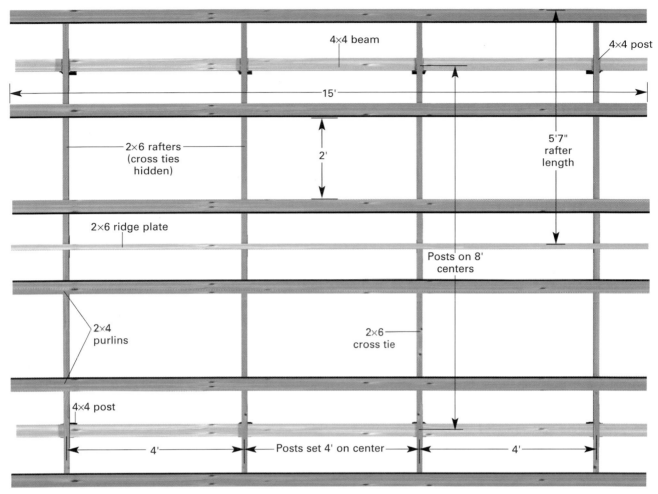

4×4 beam

4×4 post

15'

2×6 rafters
(cross ties
hidden)

2'

5'7"
rafter
length

2×6 ridge plate

Posts on 8'
centers

2×4
purlins

2×6
cross tie

4×4 post

4'

Posts set 4' on center

4'

*Two 4×4 beams run lengthwise on top of four posts. Trusses (cross ties and rafters) fastened to the beams support a ridge post for a 2×6 ridge plate. The rafters are spanned by 2×4 purlins that provide a surface for the plywood roof decking.*

## ALTERNATE FOOTING

Instead of placing posts on post anchors set in concrete footings, you can set them directly in the ground and fill the holes with concrete. Posts set this way are harder to move, remove, or repair. Buy pressure-treated (rated for ground contact) or naturally weather-resistant posts.

Dig holes 4 feet deep (or to the depth required by local codes) and 12 to 18 inches across. Add 6 inches of gravel at the bottom. Center each post in its hole and plumb it with temporary braces. Fill the postholes with concrete and check to make sure the posts are still plumb while the concrete is wet. Slope the top of the concrete with a trowel to let water run off. When the concrete has set, remove the braces.

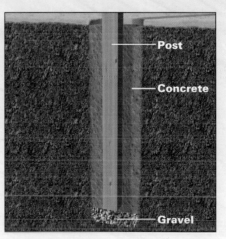

Post

Concrete

Gravel

# FREESTANDING OVERHEAD
*continued*

*Attach the rafters directly on top of the cross ties with reinforcing plates designed for that purpose. A solid roof is heavy, so it needs strong support to withstand its own weight and the weight of snow in cold climates.*

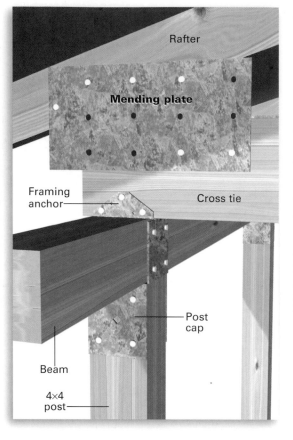

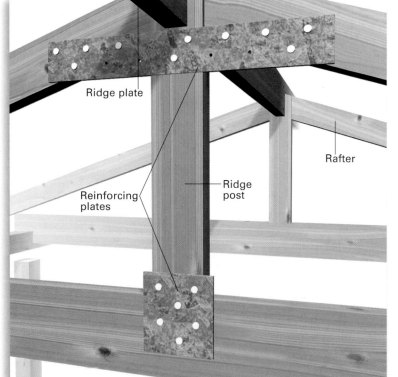

*Reinforcing plates strengthen spliced joints. The plates tie all the surfaces together as if constructed as a single piece.*

Fasten metal post caps to the tops of the posts. Cut the beams (in this design they are 15 feet long, extending beyond the posts) and set them in the post caps. Make sure the overhanging ends are evenly spaced. Fasten the beams in the caps.

If your span is longer and requires more than one beam length, butt-joint or lap-joint them centered on a post. To make a lap joint, use a hand saw to cut a 1¾×4-inch notch in the meeting ends. Overlap and nail the notches together. Whether you use lap joints or simply butt the ends together, secure the joined beams to the post with metal T-straps.

Now you're ready to build the roof frame. You can follow the steps below to build the trusses on the beams, or you can build them on the ground and set each truss assembly in place.

## CROSS TIES

Mark the locations on both beams for placing the cross ties. Make sure you measure from the same beam end. Set framing anchors at the marked locations and nail them in place.

Cut the cross ties to length (from the outside face of one beam to the other—8' 3½" in this design), then mark the midpoint of each. Set the cross ties in the anchors. The ends should be flush with the outer faces of the beams.

Nail one side of each cross tie to an anchor, then check the other end to make sure it's flush. Gently tap the beams with a hammer to make small adjustments, then finish nailing.

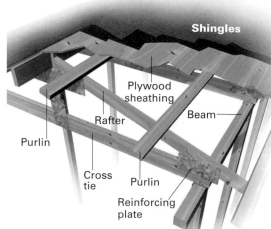

*The ridge plate rises above the rafters by 1½ inches—the thickness of the 2×4 purlins. When the purlins are installed, the sheathing sits flush against the entire roof surface.*

## RIDGE POSTS AND RAFTERS

Measure and cut the four ridge posts (2' 4¼" in this design). Point the top end at the angle you've chosen for the roof (you may have to experiment with scrap to get it right). Now cut a 1½×4-inch notch centered in the ridge posts (the ridge plate fits into this slot, leaving 1½ inches above the rafters). Toenail the bottom of the ridge posts in the center of the crossbeams and strengthen them with a reinforcing plate.

Next cut the rafters to length, angled so their top edge matches the angle of the ridge post. Attach the rafters to the ridge post with a reinforcing plate at least 4 inches below the peak. If you've built the assembly in place, you're ready for the ridge. If not, set the trusses in place and nail them to the anchors.

Cut the 2×6 ridge plate to length, and set it in the notches so its ends extend evenly. Nail through the rafters into the ridge.

## ROOF

Nail 2×4 purlins over the rafters and cover the framework with exterior-grade ½- or ⅝-inch outdoor plywood sheathing. Nail 2×2 stock on the rafters where the sheathing joints will fall. Lay 30-pound felt underlayment over the plywood, then finish the roof with composition shingles (follow the manufacturer's instructions). Roofing nails should penetrate the plywood sheathing but should not go all the way through it.

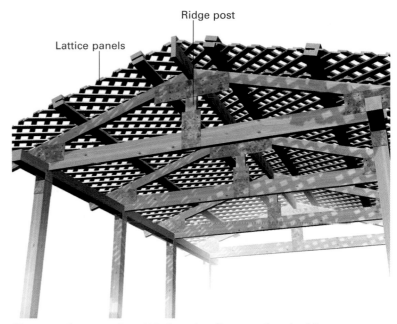

Ridge post

Lattice panels

*You can also complete this freestanding overhead with a canopy made of lattice. This provides more ventilation and works well in areas where shelter from the rain is not as important as protection from the heat or the sun.*

2×2 slats

*A canopy with slats instead of a shingled roof might allow you to use lighter lumber for beams and cross ties. Whenever you modify an existing plan, have a building inspector check and approve it before you start building.*

## MATERIALS FOR FREESTANDING OVERHEAD

| Description | Material/Size | Quantity |
|---|---|---|
| Footings | Poured concrete | 6 cu. ft.* |
| | Gravel for bottoms of holes | 100 lbs. |
| Post anchors | To hold 4×4 posts | 8 |
| Bolts for post anchors | As required, usually 2 each | 16 |
| Posts | 4×4 lumber, 8' minimum | 8 |
| Beam brackets | To hold 4×8 beam | 8 |
| Bolts for beam brackets | As required, usually 2 each | 16 |
| Beams | 4×4 lumber, 16' | 2 |
| T-straps or beam splices | To join beam boards | as needed |
| Framing anchors | To hold 2×6 cross ties | 8 |
| Cross ties | 2×6 lumber, 10' | 4 |
| Ridge posts | 2×6 lumber, 8' | 2 |
| Ridge plate | 2×6 lumber, 15' | 1 |
| Rafters | 2×4 lumber, 6' minimum | 8 |
| Metal mending plates | To attach rafters to cross ties | 8 |
| Plate straps | Galvanized steel, 24" | 4 |
| Purlins | 2×4 lumber | 90 lin. ft. |
| Sheathing | ½" or ⅝" exterior plywood, | 6 sheets |
| | or tongue-and-groove boards | 180 sq. ft. |
| Shingles | To cover sheathing | 180 sq. ft. |
| Nails | 16d HDG for 2×6 lumber | 5 lbs. |
| | 8d sinker for sheathing | 5 lbs. |
| | 8d HDG for trim | |

*Average amount; will vary by site

# ARBOR DAIS

*This arbor defines the transition from one part of the yard to another. It also provides a pleasant resting place. And it's easy to build.*

Sometimes a graceful and refined design can be sturdy and easy to build. This arbor fits that description nicely. The shaped rafters are wide dimensional lumber marked and cut in a gentle arc.

### STANDING FIRM

Some codes and some soils allow you to set posts in the ground without concrete. If you do, choose your wood carefully. Use naturally durable redwood or cedar, or pressure-treated wood rated for direct ground contact. Soak the post ends in a wood preservative so they last longer.

## POSTS

Lay out and stake the postholes according to the illustration on *page 29* using the techniques discussed on pages 10 and 14. Each pair should be centered 10½ inches apart. Dig the holes at least 4 feet deep or deeper than the frost line in your area. Pour 6 inches of gravel in each hole. Set the posts in the holes and brace them plumb (clamp 7-inch spacers between the tops).

Fill the postholes with concrete, checking often to make sure the posts stay plumb. As you make the pour, run a rod up and down in the concrete to release trapped air. Slope the top of the concrete to let water run off. Once the concrete is cured (three days to a week), mark them level (at 6 to 7 feet) and cut them to length. Then chamfer the tops.

**FRAMING PLAN**

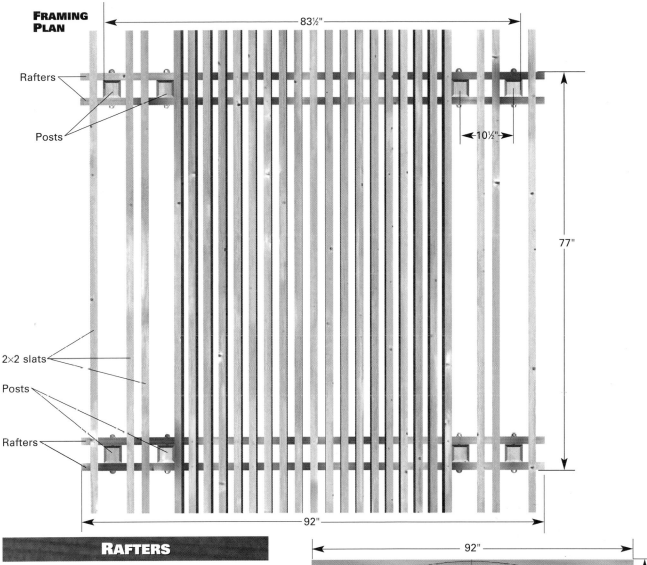

Rafters

Posts

2×2 slats

Posts

Rafters

83½"

10½"

77"

92"

## RAFTERS

Cut two rafters to length and lay them on a flat surface to form a "T." The center of the vertical rafter should be placed exactly at the center of the horizontal member.

Now loosely nail a 1×2 "compass" (slightly longer than 6 feet) in the center of the vertical piece 72 inches down from the top of the horizontal board. Drive a nail in the compass 72 inches from the pivot and scribe an arc on the horizontal rafter. From the top of the horizontal board, measure down 4 inches and from that point, another 52 inches. Move the pivot to that point and scribe a 52-inch arc. Cut the arcs with a jigsaw and smooth them with a sander. Use this rafter as a template for the others.

Tack two rafters in place. Drill holes for galvanized carriage bolts (countersink for washers and nuts on the interior rafters), centering each hole on the posts. Insert 6½-inch carriage bolts (you may have to special-order them), and fasten them.

You can vary the arcs by small amounts for a slightly different look, but each rafter should be at least 4 inches thick at its thinnest point.

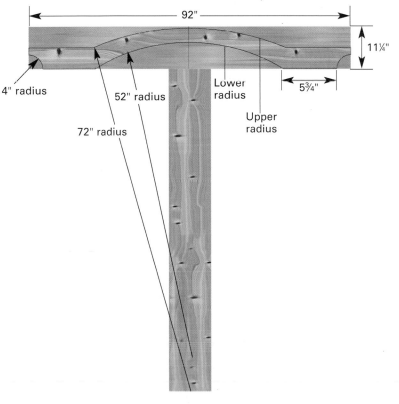

92"

11¼"

5¾"

4" radius

52" radius

Lower radius

Upper radius

72" radius

## ARBOR DAIS
*continued*

### CANOPY

The slats—like the posts and rafters—should be made of naturally weather-resistant or pressure-treated lumber. Whatever kind of lumber you've chosen for the framing, use it for the slats as well.

Slats of 2×2 lumber are available from most lumber yards and building supply centers in 8-foot lengths, and supply centers will cut them for you (if your canopy will be less than 8 feet long) for a fee. If you cut your own, cut them all before installing them. Use a power miter saw with a bench stop.

The materials list for this design specifies twenty-five 2×2 slats, but order extras in case any of the boards are warped or twisted, or if you decide to place the slats a bit closer together.

**PREDRILL:** To avoid splitting the wood, drill pilot holes in the slats. To get the holes in the same place on each slat, lay them out on a large, flat surface, such as a garage floor, and line them up against a straight edge. Measure the distance of the overhang (plus ¾ inch) and mark it on the end slats. Snap a chalk line between the marks to create a guide line for drilling the pilot holes.

**PREFINISH:** If you plan to finish the wood with stain or paint, do it now. The posts and rafters are still easy to reach, and you can coat each surface of the slats all at once. Besides, you won't want to work around all the contours of a finished arbor, even with a sprayer. By applying the finish first, you can simply touch up after installing the canopy.

Whether you stain or paint, treat the posts, rafters, and slats with a coat of preservative sealer to protect the wood.

**INSTALLING THE CANOPY:** Start the canopy by installing slats on either side of the posts. Place one slat just beyond the outside posts, two between each pair of posts, and the rest spaced evenly between the inside posts. For consistent spaces between the remaining slats, use 2×2 spacers (or a width of your choice that will space them evenly over the entire crown of the rafters).

Line up the slats so that the pilot holes are centered on the rafters. Screw the slats (with 3-inch coated deck screws) into the rafters, using the spacers to keep them in position. (Don't nail the slats—you run the risk of splitting the wood). Have a helper at the other end of the arbor, spacing and fastening as you go. Check measurements often, and adjust the spacing of the slats if necessary. As you approach the center, make small adjustments if needed for the center slat to be positioned directly overhead.

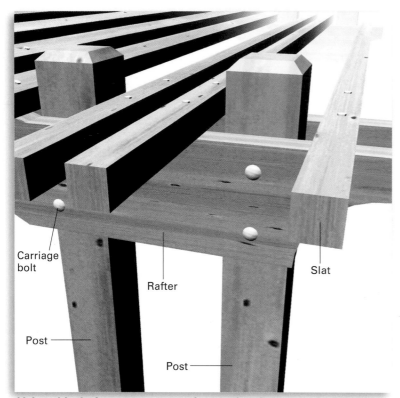

*Using this design, you can attach two slats between the outside pair of posts with slightly more than an inch of space on either side. Don't try to squeeze extra slats at the ends of the rafters. This design looks best with some visual breathing room.*

Labels on image: Carriage bolt, Rafter, Slat, Post, Post

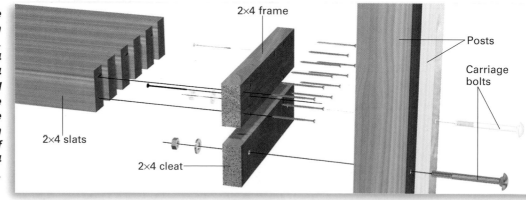

*Assemble the seat bench separately, making a 2×4 frame and 2×4 seat slats. Nail the ends to the slats and nail the assembly in place on top of the bolted 2×4 cleat.*

Labels on image: 2×4 slats, 2×4 cleat, 2×4 frame, Posts, Carriage bolts

## TO MAKE A SHORT ARBOR LONG

You can easily adapt this plan to create a long arbor, to cover a sidewalk along the side of the house, for example. Just set posts every 5 to 6 feet over the distance you wish to cover. You will need two crossbeams (rafters) for each pair of posts. If your setting requires shorter crossbeams, you will also need to alter the arcs. Experiment with the 1×2 "compass" on page 29 until you determine the upper and lower arcs (keeping the crossbeam thickness at a minimum of 4 inches). For a continuous canopy, butt joint slats directly over a crossbeam. An adapted structure such as this is ideal to support a climbing or a decorative flowering vine.

## BENCHES

To make your arbor an inviting place to stop and rest, install two facing benches between the posts. The rails and seat can be made from 2×4s and mounted at the desired height. (The average height for outdoor benches is 18 inches.) An alternative is to adapt the bench design from the shade arbor shown on page 32.

Measure the distance between the side posts (70 inches in this design). Subtract 3 inches and cut the front and rear bench rails and the seat slats to that length.

Next, measure the outside width of the paired posts (14 inches in this design). Cut the bench side rails and 2×4 cleats to that length. If you want to make the cleats decorative, scallop or notch the bottoms (no more than an inch deep).

For a bench 18 inches high, measure and mark the insides of two adjacent posts 14½ inches from the ground. For other bench heights, adjust that measurement as necessary.

Fasten a cleat on each side at this mark with two 20d nails. Mark a point 1¼ inches from the cleat end (and centered vertically on the cleat at 1¼ inch). Drill for ½-inch carriage bolts, countersinking for washers on the inside of the cleat. Install 5-inch carriage bolts. Repeat these steps for the other cleats. Seal the nuts with siliconized caulk.

Lay out the bench pieces on a flat surface and assemble them with decking screws or ring-shank nails. The dimensions of this design call for 6 seat slats for each bench, spaced about 1³⁄₁₆ inches apart (your project may require a different number of slats, but they must be set a minimum of 1³⁄₁₆ inches apart to allow for the thickness of a carpenter's hammer). Set the assembled bench seat on the cleats. Drive 16d nails through the inside of each bench end to fasten the seat to the posts.

### MATERIALS FOR ARBOR DAIS

| Description | Material/Size | Quantity |
|---|---|---|
| Footings | Concrete or packed earth | * |
| Posts | 4×4 lumber, 12' minimum | 8 |
| Rafters | 2×12 lumber, 8' | 4 |
| Bolts for rafters | 6½" galvanized carriage bolts, with washers and nuts | 16 |
| Slats | 2×2 lumber, 8' | 25 to 30 |
| Screws for benches | 3" coated decking screws | 2 lbs. |
| Bench rails and seats | 2×4 lumber, 6' | 12 |
| Bench ends and cleats | 2×4 lumber, 2' | 8 |
| Bolts for benches | 5" galvanized carriage bolts, with washers and nuts | 8 |
| Nails for benches | 10d and 20d coated | 1 lb. each |

*Will vary according to footing hole size

## FINISHING TOUCHES

For a decorative detail, tack lattice to rails toenailed between the posts, and trim the lattice edges with routed 2×2 stock. The lattice pattern will complement the overhead slats. For a greater sense of enclosure, add lattice to the short sides as well as the backs. Leave the areas below the benches open so leaves and other yard debris won't collect underneath.

Consider training vines up the posts to create a living arbor—more private perhaps, but not confining. If the vines start to overwhelm the structure, cut them back.

# SHADE ARBOR

*This pleasant arbor provides shade and privacy, yet is an open and airy garden nook for reading or contemplation.*

Lattice panels on the sides and slats overhead make this arbor a shady spot for getting away from it all. The design, size, and facing benches make it perfect for quiet conversations.

## FOOTINGS

Set up batter boards and mason's lines to establish the locations for post footings. *(For instructions, see pages 10 and 14.)* Stake the center of the footing holes and remove the lines (but not the batter boards). Dig the footing holes 12 inches wide at the top and 18 inches at the bottom and deep enough to conform to local building codes. Use a power auger or clamshell digger. If required by local codes, have the holes approved by a building inspector before pouring concrete.

Make 2×4 forms to hold concrete tube forms 1½ inches above grade. Use mason's line and a line level to make sure the forms are level. Reattach the mason's lines to the batter boards, check for square by measuring diagonals (they should be the same length), and drop a plumb bob where the strings intersect. Center each form under the plumb bob and stake the forms to keep them stable. Then mix and pour the concrete. Set post anchors, or J-bolts in the concrete while it is still wet. Recheck for centering with the plumb bob and let the concrete cure for three days to a week before going to the next steps.

## POSTS

Install post anchors on the J-bolts, set the corner posts in the anchors, and fasten them with galvanized nails. Plumb the posts with stakes and braces made of scrap 1×4s. Measure and mark one corner post to height (9 feet in this design). Use a carpenter's level, line level, or water level to mark a cut line on each corner post. Cut the posts with a circular saw. Next, install and brace the remaining posts and use a line run from the corner posts to mark cut lines. Cut the remaining posts and leave the braces in place.

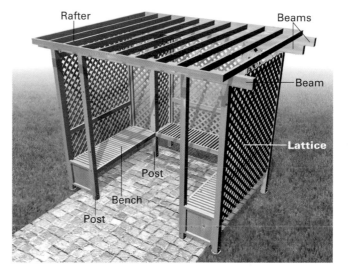

*A symmetrical design doesn't have to be plain. The straight lines and square angles of this arbor make it dignified yet not too formal.*

## BEAMS

Place metal post caps on top of all posts, aligning them so that the beams will run parallel. Fasten the post caps securely to the post with galvanized nails.

Cut the beams to length, set them into the post caps, and center them. The beam ends should extend evenly beyond the outer posts. Attach the beams to the post caps.

## RAFTERS

Assemble the frame for the rafters on the ground, but mark the end frame pieces by cutting them to length and laying them side by side, even at the ends. Mark 13-inch increments on both pieces to position the remaining rafters and assemble the frame with coated screws. To prevent splitting the ends of the rafters, predrill them.

**FRAMING PLAN**

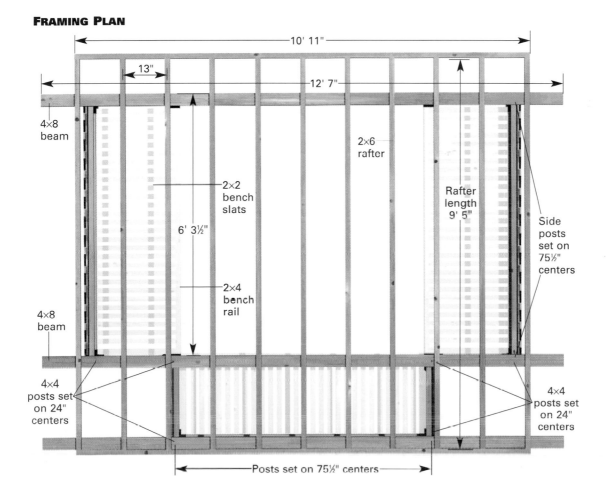

# SHADE ARBOR
*continued*

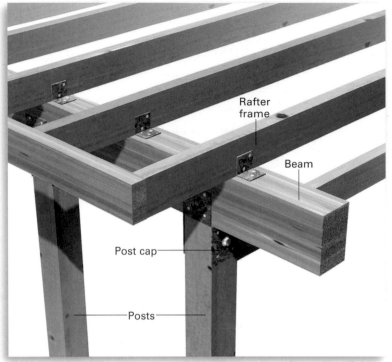

*Because the rafters do not need to support any other parts of the arbor, you can attach them to the beams with small angle brackets or framing clips. Use enough of the fasteners to hold the rafter frame securely to the beams in all kinds of weather.*

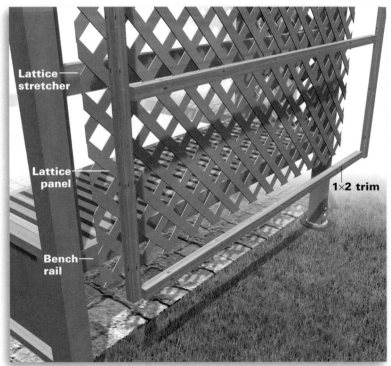

*A framework of 1×2s can hold the lattice panels in place and cover the rough edges of the lattice. Tack the lattice panels to the stretchers and the back rails of the benches with 4d nails, then attach 1×2 trim to the posts.*

Place the assembled rafter frame on top of the beams. Center it from side to side and just beyond flush at the back, or offset it by an amount you prefer—as long as it is supported by all three beams. Fasten the rafter frame to the beams with angle brackets mounted on top of the beams to keep them out of sight. Now cut and fasten the remaining rafters inside the frame at your 13-inch marks. You can use joist hangers or, to avoid showing so much hardware, nail the joists from the front and rear of the frame.

## BENCHES

Assemble the bench seats before installing them. The back rail of each bench is mounted between the posts, inset 1½ inches from the rear face to allow for the thickness of the lattice and trim. The front rail is mounted flush with the front post faces. The seat assembly is supported by a 27½-inch 2×4 cleat attached to the posts with carriage bolts. First, cut and mount the cleats 14½ inches above the ground.

Then cut the front and rear bench rails (in this design, six 72-inch 2×4s) and side rails (six 23-inch 2×4s). Assemble the bench frame as a box, with the side rails fastened inside the front and rear rails. Drill pilot holes and fasten with coated 3-inch screws.

Next, cut six 66-inch 2×2s for cleats that will support the bench slats. Nail the cleats (a nail every 8 inches) inside the front and rear rails, 1½ inches from the top of the box.

Now for the bench slats: From 2×2 stock, cut 96 slats, each 23 inches long. This job will go more quickly with a power miter or radial arm saw. Also, cut at least a half dozen 20-inch 1×2s to use as spacers.

Turn the frame top-down on a flat surface. Starting with a spacer, work alternate slats and spacers under the 1×2 cleats on the front and back rail. Make sure the pieces are square in the frame. Then predrill the cleats and slats, and fasten the slats to the cleats with 2-inch screws (use a cordless drill). Knock the spacers out with a screwdriver and repeat the process until all the slats are fastened.

Set the benches on the cleats and pin them to the posts—flush with the front—with nails or screws.

## SIDE FRAMES

Cut six 69-inch 2×4 stretchers and toenail them to the posts 42 inches from the bottom and 6 inches from the top, inset 1½ inches from the rear post face. Cut four 2×4 short stretchers and install them on the short sides, even with the long stretchers.

Slats

Post

2×4 cleat

2×2 slat cleat

Rear bench rail

*Bench slats made of 2×2s can provide comfortable seating if they are spaced closely enough. For consistent results, place scrap pieces of 1-inch-thick lumber between the seat slats as you install them. Drill pilot holes for the screws to keep the wood from splitting.*

Cut three 4×6 panels and three 2×6 panels of ready-made lattice. Center the larger panels on the bottom stretcher, and tack them to the top and bottom stretchers. Tack the smaller panels to the lower stretcher and the bench rail. Measure, cut, and tack panels for the short sides of the arbor. Cut and nail 1×2 trim to the posts on both sides of the lattice to hide its edges.

## END PANELS

Cut frames for the end panels from 2×2 stock. Nail the frames flush with the outside faces of the posts. Cut panels of marine-grade plywood to the same size as the frames. Nail the panels to the frames from the back.

2×2 Trim

End panel

Footing

*The end panels for this arbor can be finished or left open. This marine-grade plywood end hides the 2×4 bench support.*

## FINISH

Finally, decide how you want to preserve your handiwork. Finish the arbor by priming and painting or staining all exposed surfaces, depending on the look you prefer. Don't use a brush or roller for a project with this many slats and this much lattice. Buy or rent a sprayer. You won't regret it.

## MATERIALS FOR SHADE ARBOR

| Description | Material/Size | Quantity |
|---|---|---|
| Footings | Poured concrete | 8 cu. ft. avg. |
| | Gravel for base of holes | 100 lbs. |
| Post anchors | To hold 4×4 posts | 10 |
| Bolts for post anchors | As required, usually 2 each | 20 |
| Posts | 4×4 lumber, 10' minimum | 10 |
| Beam brackets | To hold 4×8 beams | 10 |
| Bolts for beam brackets | As required, usually 2 each | 20 |
| Beams | 4×8 lumber, 14' | 3 |
| Rafters | 2×6 lumber, 12' | 2 |
| | 2×6 lumber, 10' | 11 |
| Small angle brackets | To attach rafters to beams | 40 |
| Bench rails | 2×4 lumber, 6' long | 6 |
| Bench ends | 2×4 lumber, 24" | 6 |
| Bench slats | 96 2×2 lumber | 194 lin. ft. |
| Bench cleats | 2×4 lumber, 3' long | 6 |
| Cleats for bench slats | 2×2 lumber | 36 lin. ft. |
| Lattice panels | 4×8 ready-made panels | |
| Lattice trim | 2×4 lumber, 69" | 6 |
| Nails and screws | As needed | |

# ENTRY TRELLIS WITH GATE

*This inviting entry trellis provides a warm welcome for visitors. This entry works well with both shrubbery and fences. For a free-standing entry, just eliminate the gate.*

This trellis uses common lumber sizes. Its design includes the same elements as larger overhead structures, but on a smaller scale. The posts and beams are 4×4s, the top slats are 2×4s, and the decorative trim on the sides and gate can be cut from 4×8 sheets of ready-made lattice.

## ADAPTING THIS PLAN

An entry trellis can stand alone, or it can be a portal to the yard, through a fence, hedge, or garden. The fence and gate should complement each other in color, style, and materials.

A climbing vine, such as clematis or ivy, will grow eagerly along the fence. A shrub such as arborvitae is fast-growing and thick, and you can easily trim it to a pleasant shape and size. Ferns also make an attractive edging.

An alternative is to plant a flower bed on either side of the trellis. Easy-care perennials can grow and spread from the same roots each year.

## POSTS

Choose the trellis location and mark the centers of the footing holes (48 inches on center, front to back, and 44½ inches on center, side to side). Run mason's lines from diagonal stakes and measure the diagonals. Your layout is square when the measurements are equal. Dig the holes a foot wide to the depth required by local building codes. Add 6 inches of gravel in the bottom of each hole for drainage; then pour concrete. Slope the concrete to let rainwater drain off.

Set post anchors in the concrete while it is still wet (check again for square) and let the footings cure for three days to a week, depending on weather conditions. Tamp soil in any gaps at the edge of the concrete.

Set 4×4 posts in the anchors; hold them plumb with braces made from 1x4 scrap. Drill pilot holes and fasten the posts to the anchors with lag screws.

Mark one post at 84 inches. Use a carpenter's level to mark cut lines on the other posts. Then cut all the posts at the marks. Chamfer the tops with a plane for decoration.

## BEAMS

Cut two 2×4 beams to length (5 feet, 5 inches). Fasten a post cap to the top of each post, and set the beams in the post caps. Make sure they overhang the beams by the same amount.

## SIDES

This design calls for 44½-inch rails at the top, middle, and bottom of each side, but measure between your posts before cutting. Cut two sets of rails and toenail them to the posts. The top rails should be flush with the post tops and inset from the back of the posts by ¾ inch, and the bottom rail 5½ inches above the ground and flush with the back face of the posts. Toenail the middle rails flush with the back of the posts, 38 inches from the top of the top rail.

**SPINDLES:** Now cut the 1×6 spindles to 46¼ inches—eight of them for each side. Leave a ¾-inch gap between the spindles and the posts, and equal spaces between each spindle. (This will work if your measurements are the same as ours. If not, adjust your spacing or change the number of spindles.) Center the spindles on the rails and attach them with coated screws.

**LATTICE AND TRIM:** Cut 1×1 trim for the lattice frames. You'll need two 38-inch pieces and one 44½-inch piece for each side. Fasten the shorter pieces to the posts (inset ¾ inch from the back face) and the longer one to the middle rail (inset ¾ inch from the spindles).

Cut two 38×44½ lattice panels and slip the bottom of each behind the spindles and tack the panels to the top rail and side frames.

## CANOPY

Cut slats from 2×4 stock, 60 inches long. The ends of each slat should extend 5 or 6 inches beyond the side top rails. Starting at the front with a 2-inch space and using a 2× spacer between the slats, predrill the slats where they will be attached to the beams. Fasten the slats to the beams with weather-resistant screws.

## GATE

Create a frame for the gate from 2×4s. Cut the two sides 45 inches long, the top and bottom rails 41 inches long, and the middle rail 38 inches long. Assemble the frame with coated nails or wood screws. Add corner and T-brackets for greater strength.

Attach the middle rail to create the upper opening 13¼ inches high. Cut 10 spindles and nail them in the lower opening at 1-inch intervals.

Then cut 2 sets of 1×1 trim pieces (the top and bottom frames at 38 inches and the side pieces at 10¼ inches) to fit the upper opening. Attach one set to the interior of the gate frame. Cut a 13¼×38-inch piece of lattice and attach it to the trim and then install the other set of trim pieces. Hang the gate with hardware on the outside faces of the posts. Adjust the hardware as needed.

### LOCAL CODES

Remember: Before beginning any project, check local building codes for restrictions—such as maximum height or minimum setback—that might affect your plans. Don't assume that existing structures you see in your community meet local building codes.

**GATE DETAIL**

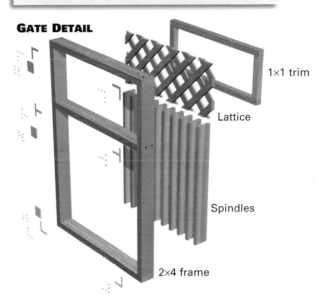

1×1 trim

Lattice

Spindles

2×4 frame

## MATERIALS FOR ENTRY TRELLIS WITH GATE

| Description | Material/Size | Quantity |
|---|---|---|
| Footings | Poured concrete | 4 cu. ft.* |
| | Gravel for bottoms of holes | 50 lbs. |
| Post anchors | To hold 4×4 posts | 4 |
| Bolts for post anchors | As required, usually 2 each | 8 |
| Posts | 4×4 lumber, 8' minimum | 4 |
| Post caps | To hold 4×4 beams | 4 |
| Bolts for post caps | As required; usually 2 each | 16 |
| Beams | 2×4 lumber, 6' | 2 |
| Top Slats | 2×4 lumber, 5-6" | 11 |
| Side rails | 2×4 lumber, 4' long | 6 |
| Side lattice | Ready-made lattice, 38"×45" | 2 |
| Side spindles | 1×6 lumber, 48" | 16 |
| Gate sides | 2×4 lumber, 4' long | 2 |
| Top and bottom gate rails | 2×4 lumber, 4' long | 2 |
| Middle gate rail | 2×4 lumber, 4' long | 1 |
| Gate lattice | Ready-made lattice, 10"×41½" | 1 |
| Gate spindles | 1×4 lumber, 3' long" | 10 |
| Trim pieces | 1×1 lumber | 120 lin. ft. |
| Nails and screws | As needed | |

*Average amount; will vary by site*

# ADAPTING OVERHEAD STRUCTURES

You can modify each plan in this book to fit other situations. By substituting trim materials, you can alter the look of an overhead structure without changing its function. You also can use heavier lumber for larger structures, or choose finishes other than the ones shown in these plans.

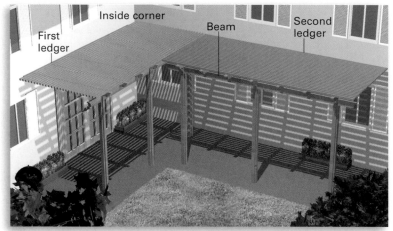

*To combine two similar structures, you may need to change the location and number of supports, such as footings and ledger boards. In this design, though, the two parts can be built separately, either at the same time or one now and the other later.*

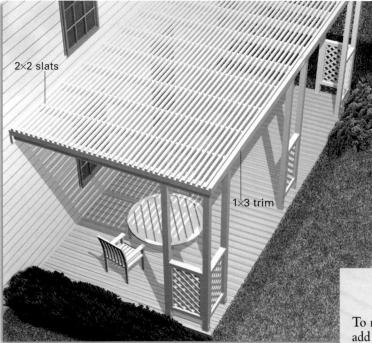

*The material you use for the canopy of a shade structure should complement the exterior of your house or other elements of your outdoor living space. These slats continue the horizontal lines of the clapboard siding, so they blend in well.*

## WRAPAROUND SHADE

The attached shade structure shown on pages 14–17 takes a different turn here. The L-shape adaptation will fit an inside or an outside corner. For an inside L, extend the ledger to the corner wall, then attach a second ledger to the adjoining wall.

Build the first structure as directed in the original plan, then build a second structure perpendicular to the first. Support the outside edge with additional posts, and tie the outside beams of the structures together with corner brackets.

## SLATS OVERHEAD

Instead of a lattice canopy for the low-profile, attached overhead (*pages 20–23*), consider using sturdy 2×2 slats. The slats give the structure a more substantial appearance, and eliminate the cross blocks used in the original design. That means less material to cut, fit, and nail.

With the framing constructed, cut 2×2 slats, predrill them, and nail them in place. Space the slats an equal distance apart from one another for a consistent appearance. For most designs, 2 to 4 inches will give you a neat-looking pattern, creating a balance between the width of the slats and the spaces. Wider spacing tends to appear unfinished. Join any splices between two lengths of slat directly over the joists for greater strength.

Prime and paint the slats before you attach them. Then you can just touch up the finish with a paint brush after installation to cover nicks and nail holes. Remember that paint usually does not last as long as stain. If you don't want to refinish your outdoor structure as often, use a sealer and stain.

Another option is to build your own lattice. Follow the instructions on page 40. Building your own offers you more creative freedom to create unique patterns, if none of the prefabricated designs suits you.

## CHANGING SIZE

To make an overhead wider, increase the joist length or add beams and posts. Longer spans may require larger framing members, especially if the structure has to support winter snow. Larger joists require larger beams and posts. To make a roof longer, increase the ledger length and add posts.

*Create a cantilevered canopy by adding beams and moving the posts.*

## CANTILEVERED CANOPY

The arbor plan on pages 28–31 can be adapted to create a cantilevered canopy to cover a shady garden spot, a child's sandbox, or even a hot tub. To build the altered plan, add 2×8 beams below the rafters to support another pair of cantilevered rafters and the extended canopy. The canopy can be longer by half the length of the original.

Build the extended canopy from shaped rafters and install predrilled slats as you would on the original. Prime and paint the slats before you attach them.

## SLAB FLOORING

You can also change your foundation. Many building codes allow you to set a freestanding overhead structure on a poured concrete slab, which also provides a dry, solid floor.

**PREPARATION:** Mark the dimensions for the slab with batter boards and mason's lines (see page 10). Stake the corners and run a line at ground level between the stakes. Mark the ground line with chalk or spray paint. Dig a perimeter trench 12 inches wide and at least 12 inches deep (or to the depth required by your local building code). Have your local building inspector sign off on the footings before you proceed.

■ **FORMS:** Use 2× lumber to build forms for the concrete. Hold the forms in place with 2×4 stakes placed at 24-inch intervals.

■ **EXCAVATION:** Excavate 8 inches of soil inside the forms and spread a 4-inch gravel bed over the enclosed area. Then lay wire reinforcing mesh (6/6,10-10) supported on and tied to 2-inch dobies (small concrete blocks made for this purpose). Now you're ready for the pour.

**POURING CONCRETE:** Compute how much concrete the slab will require in cubic yards (a cubic yard will roughly fill the area for a 9×9 slab 4 inches thick). Place your order with a local dealer for the time and date you wish to complete the slab. Call again the day before the concrete is scheduled for delivery to confirm the arrival time.

After the concrete has been poured, level the slab to the tops of the forms. Use a straight 2×4 as a screed board, and work quickly and carefully. Concrete will stiffen in one to four hours, depending on weather conditions. After the concrete has been leveled but while it is still wet, check the locations for the post anchors, and set them in place.

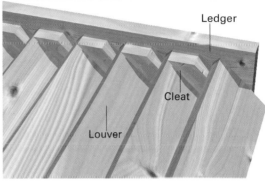

*Louvers will increase shade. Orient them to the afternoon sun. East-west slats will produce the most shade. Create equal angles and spaces for louver slats with 2×2 cleats.*

**DIRECT LIGHT AND SHADE**   **AVERAGE LIGHT AND SHADE**

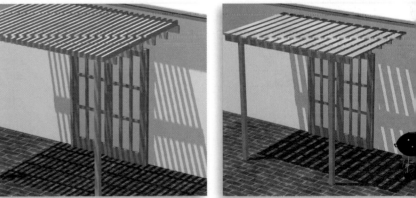

*Spacing slats the same distance as their thickness (above left) creates 50 percent shade with overhead sun. Wider slats (above right) or slats spaced more closely will increase the shade. Shade will increase as the angle of the sun changes from overhead.*

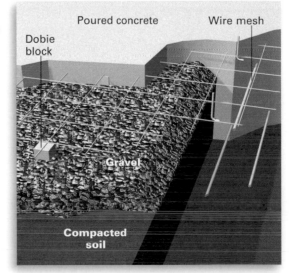

*Before you pour a concrete slab for a foundation, check with your local building department to see how thick the slab needs to be because of the climate in your area. A failed concrete slab is a problem you want to avoid.*

## ADAPTING OVERHEAD STRUCTURES
*continued*

*Sometimes smaller is better. By taking one part of a larger plan and building it separately, you can create a structure that fits within available smaller spaces. The flowering shrubs and hedge that surround this arbor make it a subtle accent in an out-of-the-way spot. You can adapt the shade arbor plan in other ways as well.*

### SMALL-SCALE SHADER

Shrink the garden shade arbor (*see pages 32-35*) to fit a small space by leaving off the sides. Construction now involves only four posts and one cozy bench, with the back and sides covered by a lattice mesh.

This easy-to-build variation offers further options for change. For example, you can replace the lattice—which provides shade but has no structural purpose—with slats, louvers, or other material you think would look better or last longer in your setting.

The arbor's overhead surface should be ventilated to prevent water from collecting and damaging the wood, and to reduce snow buildup. Use just enough material at the top to provide shade at noon.

Remember that the scale of a small yard or garden can be overpowered by a massive wooden structure. To keep the arbor unobtrusive, set it back from high-traffic areas and finish it with a stain or paint that lets it blend well with the surrounding landscape.

Two shade arbors, built to face each other, can create a pleasant spot for relaxation and conversation along a garden pathway.

## HOW TO MAKE LATTICE

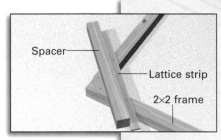

Spacer
Lattice strip
2×2 frame

Second layer    First layer

Trim with circular saw

Many shade-structures call for lattice. You can buy it premade in various sizes and shapes at most building centers. But if you want to make your own, here's how:

■ Start with a simple frame of 2×2 stock, making sure the corners are square. The frame will be part of the finished lattice and should fit snugly into its opening.

■ Cut a piece of lattice strip to extend across one corner.

■ With wire brads or staples, attach the lattice strip to the frame. For large projects, use a rented power stapler—you'll spend a little more but save yourself hours of time in the long run.

■ Using a spacer to create a gap between the lattice strips, install the rest of the lattice.

■ Next, repeat the process, laying the second group of lattice pieces in the opposite direction from the first. Make sure the first piece of the second layer is at right angles to the first layer, and check yourself as you continue laying the lattice.

■ Cut off the overhanging ends of the lattice pieces so that they are flush with the outside edges of the frame. Set the circular saw just to the depth of the lattice to avoid scarring the frame

■ Nail 2×2 framing to the opposite side and install the assembly in the opening of your structure.

■ To simplify the installation, paint or stain the lattice strips and frame before you assemble the pieces. The finished lattice and frame should be ready to install.

## MAKING ROOM

The trellis entry (*see pages 36–37*) can be adapted to include a short bench or shelves for potted plants. This variation makes the trellis both functional and decorative.

Add a second row of posts to a bench. Use the instructions for benches with the shade arbor (*see pages 34–35 and below*), adapting the plan for the measurements of your trellis. To add a second bench or opposite shelving, add two more posts.

Shelving, of course, can be added to both sides of the entry. Build shelves in much the same way as benches, with solid surfaces to hold smaller items, or with slats for ventilation. For each shelf, construct a frame of 2×4s to match the inside dimensions of the trellis. Center the frame inside the posts at the desired height, and tack it in place with nails from the inside. Check the shelf for level, drill and countersink pilot holes, and attach the shelf with lag screws. Or, to preserve the appearance of the posts, use metal angle brackets for shelf supports.

*One structure can incorporate elements of two or more others. This design combines a trellis with a gate, a shade arbor, and a storage shed with shelves. The result will be a structure that's uniquely yours, and one that does just what you want.*

## ADDING BENCHES

You can adapt some of the designs in this book to include built-in seating like the three examples shown here. All that's required is taking advantage of posts or other supporting members.

Build a bench frame from 2×4 or 2×6 lumber, set on edge and fastened between the posts of an overhead structure. To create the strongest joints, use metal angle brackets and galvanized or coated wood screws to attach the bench frame parts to the posts.

Another option is to attach cleats made of 2×6 or 2×8 lumber to the inside edges of the posts with carriage bolts, then set the ends of the bench slats on the cleats.

Benches that are 15 to 18 inches high and 15 to 18 inches deep are comfortable for most people. You can make the seats even deeper if you intend to add a lounge pad. For

that matter, you can build a bench as shallow as 12 inches if you expect to use it more as a temporary resting spot than a hideaway for novel-reading.

Allow for kickspace underneath, and support the bench with legs if it is wider than 3 feet.

Chamfer the front edges of the bench to remove sharp corners and to add a nice finishing touch.

Bench frame with brace

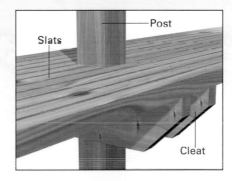

Post
Slats
Cleat

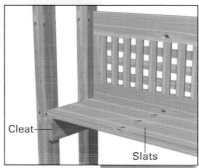

Cleat
Slats

Nestled under a shade tree, this weathered shed is an extension of the surrounding landscape. The open cantilever lends a light feeling despite its heavy beams, and the unfinished naturally resistant wood has developed character with age. Composition shingles complement the rough-and-tumble look of the shed, and the dry-stacked stone wall and vines complete the contrasts.

# HARD-WORKING SHEDS

*Sheds have an image to maintain—a sense that they always have a job to do. Their work is seldom glamorous and never done. Sheds are usually occupied, but quietly, by something if not someone. After all, if they were busier, they'd be workshops. It can be argued that a shed is just a shop that lacks ambition. In the realm of busy backyards, shops produce things; sheds maintain them.*

*A shed is a big closet without the fuss of wrapping a house around it. Sheds have an easy-going personality, with a built-in commitment to service without pretense. They safely house the tools you need and the toys you enjoy. And, if you're industrious, they'll even offer space for some garden puttering or do-it-yourself projects. No wonder books have been devoted to the faithful, versatile shed.*

*This chapter showcases six sheds that reflect the versatility of styles and purposes. You can build any of them as shown, of course. But don't restrict your imagination. The plans on these pages may inspire something uniquely your own. And an hour at the hardware store can yield a shopping cart loaded with brackets and racks and gadgets to boost the capacity of the lowliest shed.*

*Finally, no matter how modest its purpose, build something you'll take satisfaction in seeing. Although the shed you have in mind is for storage, work, play, or gardening, it doesn't have to look like a utilitarian structure. A well-designed shed—like any of the designs presented here—will complement its surroundings and help increase the value of your home. More importantly, it will continue to enhance your enjoyment of it.*

## DETERMINING YOUR NEEDS

Before settling on a specific design for your shed, take time to think about what purpose you want the finished structure to serve.

### STORAGE
■ Storage bins can hold nails, screws, and other small hardware items within easy reach.
■ Drawers, cabinets, shelves, and wall hangers make tools easier to find, take out, and put back.
■ Ceiling hangers and shelves are available in sizes that hold bikes and camping equipment neatly and safely.

### WORK SPACE
■ A workbench offers a regular place to work on household repair tasks without disrupting other activities; enclosing it in a shed lets you tackle long-term projects.

### GARDENING
■ A potting bench provides a place to start seedlings, and to keep smaller gardening supplies.
■ Shelves can help keep pots and garden tools handy, and bins or cabinets can store bulky items.
■ You can keep a supply of potting soil in a large plastic garbage container and store it under a potting bench.

### UTILITIES AND CONVENIENCE
■ To use the shed as a work space, you will need to provide electric service for lights and power tools.
■ For convenience, add plumbing to simplify cleaning chores and gardening tasks.
■ Add a ramp at the entrance to roll lawn and garden equipment in and out easily.

# CLASSIC AND BASIC

*This basic shed rests on foundation skids, but it could be built on a concrete slab, as well. By using materials that complement your home and other features of your landscape, you can make this utilitarian structure blend beautifully into its surroundings.*

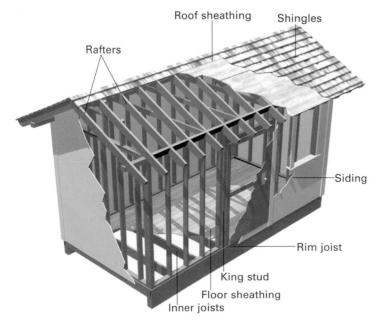

Roof sheathing

Shingles

Rafters

Siding

Rim joist

King stud

Floor sheathing

Inner joists

This versatile yard and garden shed is built with a fundamental design, which makes its construction easy. Make sure all your building materials are rated for outdoor use. The lumber in the floor frame should be pressure treated, and the foundation skids should be rated for direct ground contact.

Before you start (or at least before you begin building the walls), a little preparation is in order. You'll need to know the exact dimensions of the rough openings for windows (and for manufactured doors, if you're not building your own). If you haven't received the units yet, ask your supplier for these measurements.

## SITE LAYOUT

Set up batter boards and mason's lines to lay out the 8×16-foot site (see *page 10* for layout information), squaring the area, and marking the excavation line with chalk or paint.

Excavate the area to a depth of 9 inches and extend the excavation at the four corners by digging foot-long trenches (for the skid ends) that are 3½ inches wide. Pour enough gravel (a little over 3 inches) in the excavated site and in the trenches, to put the height of your skids about 1½ inches above grade. Level the gravel with a garden rake, and lay landscape fabric over the gravel to keep weeds from growing through the floor.

## FOUNDATION SKIDS

Make each 18-foot foundation skid from three 2×8s nailed together flush on all four sides. Fasten them at 12-inch intervals with two 16d hot-dipped galvanized (HDG) nails or 3-inch coated decking screws.

Now set the skids in the trenches and maneuver them until they're level. Add or remove gravel under the skids to adjust them, making sure the outer edges are 8 feet apart.

## FLOOR FRAME

Assemble the floor frame off-site on a flat surface. Measure and cut the rim and floor joists to length, 16 feet and 93 inches respectively. Clamp—or have a helper hold—the rim joists flush at the ends, and mark both at 16-inch intervals; you'll use these marks later for joist-placement.

Line up the end joists so they are inside the rim joists and fasten them with three 16d nails at each corner.

Set the floor frame on top of the skids (you'll need help for this) and measure the diagonals to make sure the "box" is square. Then toenail the floor frame to the skids every 12 inches with 16d nails.

With the frame securely in place, attach the remaining joists at the 16-inch marks, using joist hangers or by nailing into the joist-ends through the rim joists.

## FLOOR DECKING

Four 4×8-foot sheets of ⅝- or ¾-inch plywood will cover the floor frame exactly. But don't lay them down without staggering the joints. Staggered joints make the structure stronger.

You also should leave a ¹⁄₁₆-inch gap between the panel ends and a ⅛-inch gap along their side edges to allow for expansion. Allow this spacing as you lay the floor, and cut off excess along the perimeter. Or run a circular saw between the joints after you lay the sheets.

■ Lay two panels end-to-end on one rim joist. Together they will cover one-half the width of the floor. Fasten these sheets with 8d nails every 6 inches at the edges and every 10 inches on the interior of each sheet.

■ Cut a 4×8 sheet in half and nail one of the halves at a corner. Lay the full sheet next and the remaining half-sheet in the other corner.

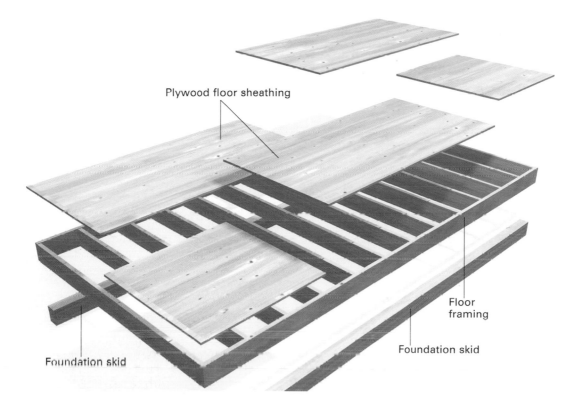

Plywood floor sheathing

Floor framing

Foundation skid

Foundation skid

*The plywood floor is supported by 2×8 floor joists set 16 inches on center. To attach the floor frame to a cement slab (instead of skids), insert anchors in the wet concrete every 4 feet, then fasten the frame to these anchors.*

# CLASSIC AND BASIC
*continued*

**WALL FRAMING**

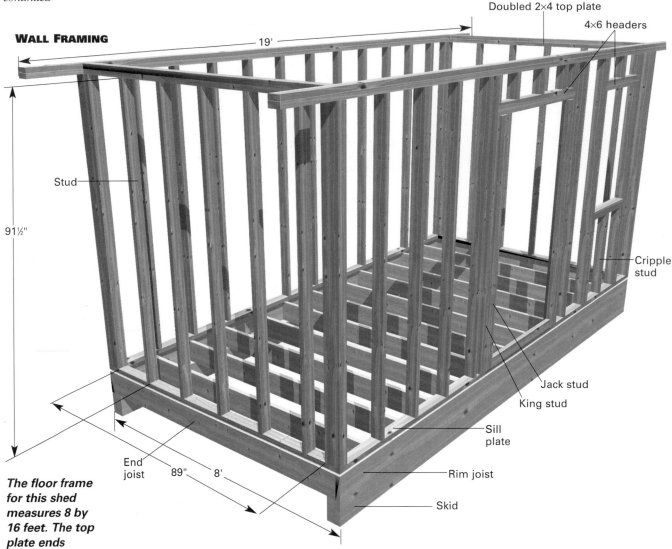

Doubled 2×4 top plate

4×6 headers

19'

91½"

Stud

Cripple stud

Jack stud

King stud

End joint

89"    8'

Sill plate

Rim joist

Skid

*The floor frame for this shed measures 8 by 16 feet. The top plate ends extend 18 inches past the studs for the roof overhang.*

## WALL FRAMING

Walls consist of a 2×4 sill plate, a doubled 2×4 top plate, and studs set 16 inches on center. Corners are tied with angle brackets.

Even if you haven't received the doors and windows yet, you need to know the exact rough opening requirements. These measurements vary among manufacturers—be certain before you build.

Assemble the front wall on a flat surface, such as the decking you just laid.

■ Cut the plates and 54 studs to length (studs at 91½ inches), but save the headers, jack, and cripple studs—for the door and window—for later.

■ Mark both plates at 16-inch intervals for stud and rafter locations, leaving openings for the door and window.

■ Attach the sill plate to the studs with 16d nails driven through the bottom.

■ Attach the bottom half of the 2×4 top plate to the studs with 16d nails. Then fasten the top half.

**WINDOW AND DOOR FRAMES:**
■ Using the rough measurements of the window opening, mark the king studs for the lower edge of the header.

■ Then, cut jack studs to that length and nail them to the king studs.

■ Measure for the lower edge of the window opening, and cut and attach the lower window ledge (toenail it to the jack stud) and lower cripple studs.

■ Cut the header to length, set it on the jack studs, and attach it by nailing through the king stud.

■ Measure, cut, and toenail the upper cripple studs in place.

Build the door frame in the same order.

**RAISING THE WALL:** With a helper, raise the wall assembly in place and nail the sill plate through the flooring to the joists with 16d nails. Then attach temporary 1×6 bracing on the side of the walls and joists. Adjust the bracing until the wall is plumb. Leave the bracing in place until the roof structure is complete or until you're ready to side the structure—whatever you do first.

■ Assemble the other three walls using the same methods. Note that the side walls fit inside the front and back walls, so the top and sill plates are cut to 89 inches each. Set and brace them in place, then plumb and fasten them.

■ Tie the corners at the top with metal corner brackets.

■ To reinforce the walls while you build the rafters, tie the corners with diagonal 2×4 braces nailed to the bottom of the top plates.

Now you can install the siding or the roof framing.

## SIDING

This shed plan uses sheets of either finished or rough-sawn, exterior-grade plywood as the siding. The plywood adds lateral strength; it helps keep the shed from falling over. If you plan to finish the shed in lapped siding, you must still install plywood sheathing.

■ Run the siding from the bottom of the floor frame to the top of the wall plates.

■ Use 8d HDG nails spaced 6 inches apart on the edges, 12 inches apart across the surface.

■ To mark the window and door openings, drive nails from the inside at the corners, snap a chalk line between the nails on the exterior, drill starter holes large enough for a saber saw blade, and cut the openings. Enlarge the openings by ½ inch with a circular saw set at the depth of the siding to allow for expansion.

## WINDOW

Windows are available in many materials and designs. The specifications for this shed include an aluminum nail-on window. Aluminum windows are easy to find and install—and are relatively inexpensive.

■ Center the window in the rough opening and shim it from inside at the nail holes on the bottom and sides until it's plumb and level. Fasten the window through the shims. Then score the shims at the frame edge with a utility knife and break them off.

■ Caulk the outside edges of the window with silicone caulk, and install exterior framing if it is not part of the manufactured unit that you ordered.

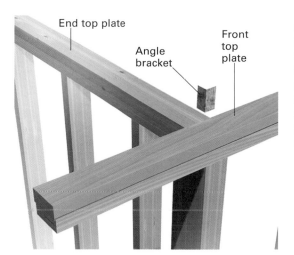

End top plate

Angle bracket

Front top plate

*Angle brackets tie the corners of the shed together and give it increased resistance against structural twisting.*

*Almost any kind of siding will work on a shed. Choose siding materials to complement your outdoor living area, and use sheathing underneath.*

*After you install the siding, add one or more windows to fit rough openings you made in the wall frame. Aluminum nail-on windows can be installed from one side; other models fasten both inside and out.*

# CLASSIC AND BASIC
*continued*

## ROOF FRAMING

The first two 2×6 rafters you cut will be the most difficult. Once you get them cut right, the rest will be easy. Mark and cut (recheck everything before you cut) the first rafter according to the pattern, *below*. Use this rafter as a template to mark and cut a second one.

■ On a flat surface, make a "mock up" of the peak by holding the rafters against a 2×6 board; a temporary stand-in for the ridge. The distance between the rafter notches should be equal to the inside width of the wall frame; 89 inches in this design. If it's not, recheck measurements and cut again. If everything works, cut the remaining rafters. Remember, the end rafters are ¾ inch longer than the others—they cover the ridge ends.

■ Cut the ridge board to length (at 18 feet, 9 inches to create a 16½-inch overhang). Mark the ridge and top plates for rafter locations—flush with the outside walls at the ends and the rest 24 inches on center.

■ Cut the 2×6 blocking that will fit between the rafters. The end pieces will be 13¾ inches long and the rest 14½ inches long.

■ Installing the rafters will be difficult at first, but you'll get the hang of it as you nail more pieces in place. First, make two 2×6 ridge braces with a 1½×5-inch notch centered in one end. You can also tack 1× stock to make a "saddle" for the ridge to rest in. Either way, tack the brace to the top plate so that the ridge will be centered on the wall and peaked at 28¾ inches above the top plate.

■ Set the ridge in the notch or saddle and make sure it overhangs each end by the same length. While a helper holds an end rafter against the ridge, toenail the rafter to the top plate with 16d nails—flush with the outside wall. Then your assistant can facenail the rafter to the ridge. Attach rafters on the opposite end the same way.

■ Check the height of the ridge to make sure the angles still work, with rafter ends snug against the ridge board; adjust it if needed.

■ Add the remaining rafters in pairs and nail the 2×6 blocking as you go.

■ Cut three 2×4 collar ties, each 8 feet long. Nail them to the fourth, sixth, eighth and tenth pairs of rafters with three 16d nails at each end. These keep the weight of the roof from spreading the walls apart.

**RAFTER LAYOUT**

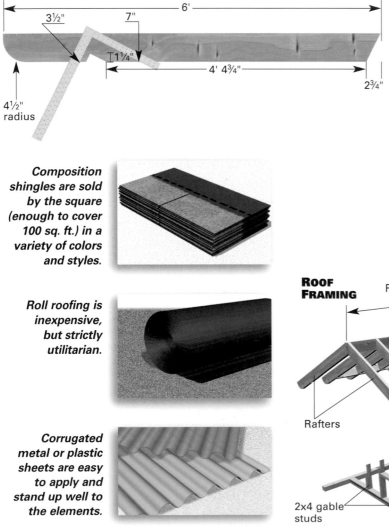

6'
3½"
7"
1¼"
4' 4¾"
2¾"
4½" radius

*Composition shingles are sold by the square (enough to cover 100 sq. ft.) in a variety of colors and styles.*

*Roll roofing is inexpensive, but strictly utilitarian.*

*Corrugated metal or plastic sheets are easy to apply and stand up well to the elements.*

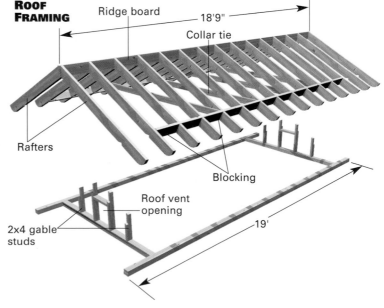

**ROOF FRAMING**

Ridge board
18'9"
Collar tie
Rafters
Blocking
Roof vent opening
2x4 gable studs
19'

■ Remove the 2×6 ridge braces and install gable rafters covering the ends of the ridge.

## ROOF COVERING

With the rafters installed, lay ½-inch or ⅝-inch plywood roof sheathing; ⅝-inch will keep roofing nails from showing in your ceiling. Arrange the sheathing so its joints are staggered, and leave the same spacing between edges as you did in the flooring. You can also sheathe the roof with oriented strand board (OSB). This material expands more than plywood, so increase the end spacing to ⅛ inch and the edge spacing to ¼ inch. To ease the task of roofing, install OSB textured side up—the finished side is extremely slick, especially with a film of sawdust. Fasten the sheathing with 8d nails every 6 inches on the edges and every 12 inches across the surface.

■ To cover the edge of the plywood and add support to the rafter tails, finish the roof edge with 1×2 cedar or redwood trim.

■ Choose a roofing material, such as composition shingles, and install it according to the manufacturer's directions.

## DOOR

This shed has one door. You can install a manufactured door or build one yourself.

■ To build your own door, make a 2×4 frame to fit the opening and reinforce it (*see page 53*) with a 2×4 diagonal at opposite corners.

■ Apply a bead of construction cement to the outer edges of the frame; then nail exterior grade plywood to the frame.

■ Hang the door with strap hinges, and install a knob or gate latch.

Most pre-hung doors are sold without a handle or latch, so you will need to install one. Add a lock so that your shed's contents will be safe.

## FINISHING TOUCHES

■ Install 1×4 trim around window and door frames.

■ Paint or stain the exterior surfaces with colors that complement the overall color scheme of your landscape and house.

■ Build a ramp for easy equipment access.

■ Install gable vents and gable studs at each end. Make gable studs of 2×4s nailed perpendicular to the top plate and notched at the roof angle. Hold them in place and mark your lines for notch cuts.

## MATERIALS FOR A BASIC SHED

| Description | Material/Size | Quantity |
|---|---|---|
| Foundation | ¾" gravel | 2 cu. yd. |
| Skids | 2×8 lumber, 18' | 6 |
| Rim joists | 2×8 lumber, 16' | 2 |
| Joists | 2×8 lumber, 8' | 13 |
| Floor sheathing | ⅝" or ¾" exterior-grade plywood, 4×8 sheets | 4 |
| Wall sill plates | 2×4 lumber, 16' | 3 |
| Wall top plates | 2×4 lumber, 20' | 4 |
| | 2×4 lumber, 8' | 4 |
| Wall studs | 2×4 lumber, 8' | 54 |
| Headers | 4×6 lumber, 8' | 1 |
| Siding | 1'×6' clapboard siding or 4'×9' plywood siding | 470 sq. ft. |
| Window | Aluminum nail-on, 4'×4' | 1 |
| Door | Pre-hung or built | 1 |
| | 2×4 lumber 8' | 2 |
| | 2×4 lumber 12' | 1 |
| Rafters and blocking | 2×6 lumber, 14' | 15 |
| Ridge board | 1×6 lumber, 20' | 1 |
| Collar ties | 2×4 lumber, 8' | 3 |
| Roof sheathing | ½" or ⅝" exterior-grade plywood, 4×8 sheets | 7 |
| Roofing | Roll roofing or composition shingles | 133 sq. ft. |
| Gable vents | 14"×14" louvered vent | 2 |
| Trim | 1×4, random lengths | 120 lin ft |
| | 1×2 lumber | 72 lin. ft. |
| Nails | 16d HDG | 2 lb. |
| | 16d sinker | 12 lb. |
| | 8d HDG | 5 lb. |
| | 8d sinker | 5 lb. |

## RAMP

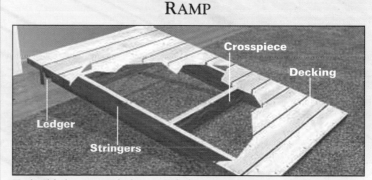

To build this ramp, bolt a 2×6 ledger to the rim joist. Attach joist hangers to the ledger and fasten 2×6 stringers (with their ends cut to fit flat on the ground) in the hangers. Attach a 2×6 crosspiece midway up the ramp. Screw 2×6 decking onto the stringers.

# SHALLOW YARDKEEPER

*This small, inexpensive shed is designed for simplicity, we've minimized the number of framing members. Use 3-inch screws instead of nails—they won't become loose or let the structure sag.*

Got a narrow stretch of yard with no particular purpose? And you need a place to store stuff, too? This shallow-profile shed is tailor-made for your situation. It's easy to build and big enough for four trash cans, a lawn mower, a bundle of rakes—and an assortment of things there never seems to be a place for.

### FLOOR

Why mess with mud? Build this shed over a concrete slab, gravel, or pavers set in sand. Excavate and finish these foundations before setting the posts.

### POSTS AND PLATES

This shed design gets its lateral stability from well-set posts. Lay out their locations according to the procedures shown on page 10, using the diagram on page 52.

■ Dig postholes 3 to 4 feet deep and a foot wide; use a clamshell digger or rent a power auger. Pour 4 inches of gravel in the bottom. Insert the corner posts in the holes (avoid scraping too much soil into the hole). Using a carpenter's level, brace them plumb (with 1×4s) at the intersection of the mason's lines.

■ Now pour concrete to the top of the holes and slope the surface to let rain water drain.

■ Set each of the middle posts in the same fashion, making sure their outer surfaces just touch the mason's lines. Let the concrete cure for three days to a week.

**TRUSS DIAGRAM**

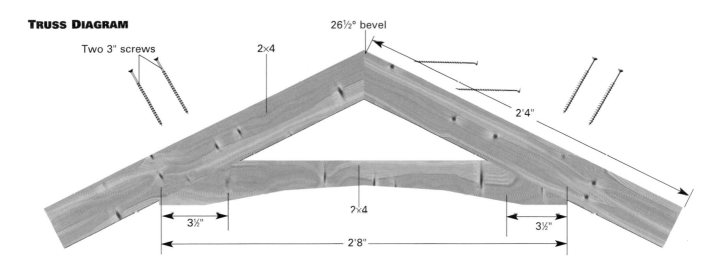

Two 3" screws

2×4

26½° bevel

2'4"

3½"

2×4

3½"

2'8"

■ After the concrete sets, mark the posts and cut them to a uniform height of 6 feet, 4½ inches (use a water level or carpenter's level after the first cut—don't measure from the ground each time). Then fasten the 2×4 plates (12 feet, 6 inches long) to the top of the front and rear posts, using three 3-inch screws per post. Pull any stray posts into alignment as you fasten the plates.

the purlins with ³/₄×8 pan head sheet-metal screws (with rubber washers, if you can find them), overlapping the sheets by one corrugation. Cover the ridge with two beveled 1×6 cap, 12 feet, 9¾ inches long, attached to the purlins with 3-inch screws.

## ROOF

**TRUSSES:** To construct the roof, first assemble the four roof trusses on a flat surface (*see diagram above*). Cut the arc (the arc is optional, of course) with a scroll saw and smooth it with a sander. Then attach the trusses to the plates with angle brackets centered over the posts.

**PURLINS:** Next, cut the six 2×2 purlins (horizontal roof members) to 12 feet, 6 inches. Fasten the purlins to the roof trusses with screws.

**PANELS:** This design calls for ribbed fiberglass sheeting, but metal roofing or ½-inch plywood and conventional shingles would work just fine. To install a fiberglass roof, cut the panels (with a fine-toothed blade) so they overhang the lower purlin by about an inch. Next, attach the sheets to

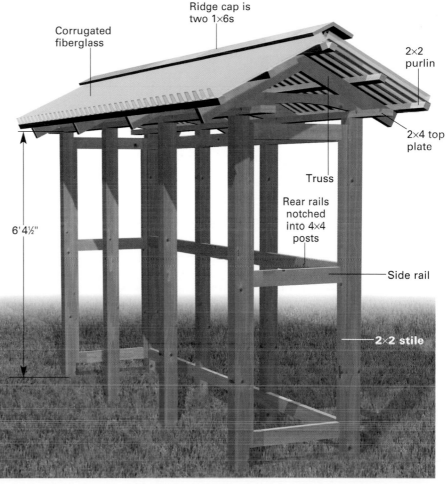

Ridge cap is two 1×6s

Corrugated fiberglass

2×2 purlin

2×4 top plate

Truss

Rear rails notched into 4×4 posts

Side rail

6'4½"

2×2 stile

## SHALLOW YARDKEEPER
*continued*

### FRAMING DESIGN

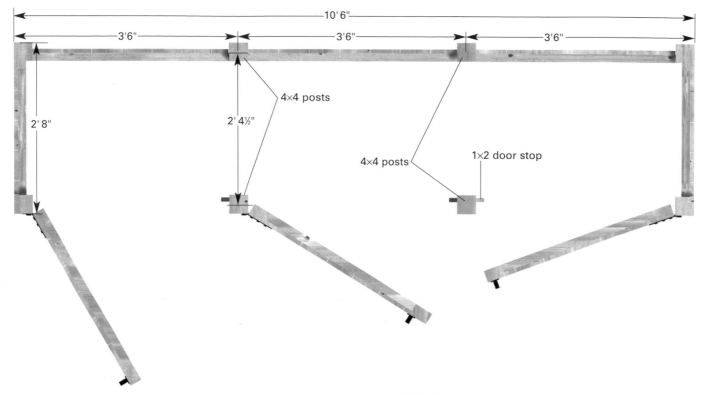

### BACK AND SIDE WALL FRAMING

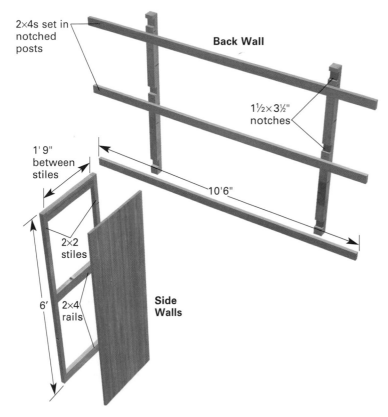

2×4s set in notched posts

Back Wall

1½×3½" notches

1' 9" between stiles

10'6"

2×2 stiles

6'　2×4 rails

Side Walls

---

### WALLS

As shown, we've left the eaves and ends of the shed open at the top and bottom to provide ventilation for trash cans. You can enclose the shed if you have critters around that might view the rubbish as a buffet. Extend the siding and door to ground level and tack wire mesh in the open spaces at the top. In either case, build the back wall first.

**NOTCHING THE RAILS:** Cut three 10½-foot 2×4 rails. Then notch each rear post at 4 inches above the ground (bottom edge of the bottom rail) and 3 inches below the top plate, measured from the top of the top plate to the top of the notch. The posts are notched for the middle rail at mid point. All the notches are 1½×3½ inches, and cutting them is easy. Here's how:

■ Set your circular saw at 1½ inches and make several cuts about ¼ inch apart.

■ Knock out the remaining waste with a hammer, and smooth the edges of the notch with a chisel.

■ Fit the rails into the notches and attach them with two 3-inch screws. To make the work easier, drill pilot holes for the screws.

**EASY SIDE WALLS:** Construction of the side walls is easier. Instead of notching posts to hold rails, simply assemble 2×2 frames on a flat surface and install them between the side posts as completed units.

■ Measure the distance between the side posts (25 inches in our installation), cut the side rails 3 inches shorter—to account for the thickness of the stiles—and cut the stiles to length (at 6 feet). Assemble the panels.

■ Next, place the assembled panels between the side posts, lined up with the bottom rails, and fasten them in place— flush with the inside corners of the posts— by driving screws through the stiles and into the posts.

**SIDING:** When you have attached the rail and frames to the walls, you're ready to add siding to the frame. Side the shed with shiplap, tongue and groove, or ordinary fence boards. To avoid an uneven appearance, measure and plan so that the first and last pieces in each wall panel are at least a half board wide.

■ Cut siding panels to length (here, 6 feet).

■ Drill pilot holes to avoid splitting the siding and fasten it to the rails with screws. Use two 2-inch screws at each end for 1×6 stock, or three screws for 1×8s or wider. Screws are easier to remove than nails if you need to repair or replace siding.

## DOORS

The simple door for this design is made of siding screwed to a Z-shape 2×4 frame about ½ inch narrower than the actual opening to allow for expansion.

■ To build it, cut the framing members to length and assemble them on a flat surface. Note that the end doors are slightly narrower than the center door shown above right. Measure your openings to be sure.

■ Screw the stiles to the top and bottom rails. Then mark and cut a diagonal brace and screw it in place.

■ Attach T-hinges and gate latches to each door, then hang the doors by fastening the hinges to the post.

■ Finish by mounting a 6-foot, 1×2 stop on the inside of the latch post.

## FINISHING

■ Protect all the exposed surface with paint, stain, or preservative sealer.

■ Install shelving in the upper half of the shed to give you extra storage of small items. Leave the bottom area open for larger stuff— lawn mowers and refuse cans.

■ Don't forget that hangers and hooks will keep rakes, shovels, and other long-handled tools from getting tangled up in corners.

6'

3' 2½"

**CENTER DOOR DIMENSIONS**

*A sturdy Z-frame door made from 2×4s will hang from T-hinges and not sag under its own weight. Add latches and locks that match the shed's style.*

### MATERIALS FOR SHALLOW YARDKEEPER

| Description | Material | Size | Quantity |
|---|---|---|---|
| Post footings | Concrete | | ⅓ cu. yd. |
| Lumber | Posts | 4×4 lumber, *10' minimum | 8 |
| | Rails, trusses | 2×4 lumber, 12' | 8 |
| | Plates | 2×4 lumber, 14' | 2 |
| | Gate frames | 2×4 lumber, 8' | 12 |
| | Purlins | 2×2 lumber, 14' | 6 |
| Roof | Roofing panels | 2×8 fiberglass panels | 4 |
| | Ridge cap | 1×6 lumber, *14' | 2 |
| Siding | Boards | 1×6 lumber | 58 pieces |
| Hardware | Screws | 3½" coated deck screws | 1½ lbs. |
| | | 1⅜" coated deck screws | 2 lbs. |
| | | ¼×8" sheet metal screws | 100 ea. |
| Assorted metal fasteners per text | | | |

*Cedar, redwood, cypress, or pressure-treated*

# LOW-SLUNG STOWAWAY

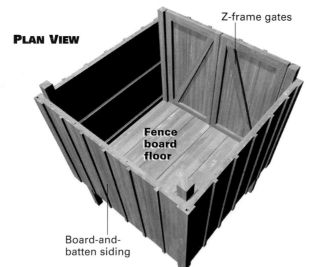

**PLAN VIEW**

Z-frame gates

Fence board floor

Board-and-batten siding

At just 7½ feet tall, this stalwart stub of a garden shed is ideal where zoning restricts building height or where the scale of a taller shed might dwarf surrounding landscape features. Use naturally decay-resistant wood, such as redwood or cedar, or pressure-treated lumber. The posts should be rated for ground contact.

## LAYOUT AND POST SETTING

Using the diagram on *page 55*, lay out the site with batter boards and mason's line (see *page 10* for more information), squaring diagonals and marking the center of posthole footings. Dig the holes—12 to 18 inches wide and 2 to 3 feet deep—and pour in 6 inches of gravel. Set the posts in, plumb them with temporary braces, and fill the holes with concrete, sloping the surface to promote drainage. Let the concrete cure for three days to a week.

## FRAME AND FLOOR

Level the ground (see "Setting the Gravel Base," *below*), lay landscape fabric to keep the weeds down, and spread a layer of coarse gravel. Tamp the gravel to a consistent 3-inch depth. Cut all joists to length. Set the side and rear rim joists directly on top of the gravel and nail them to the outside edges of the posts with 16d nails. Nail the front joist (at gravel level also) to the interior of the front posts and inset from the front face by the thickness of the door material—¾ to 1 inch, depending on the material you use. Nail the remaining joists 17 inches on center. Finally, install the floor boards (notch the boards at the corners).

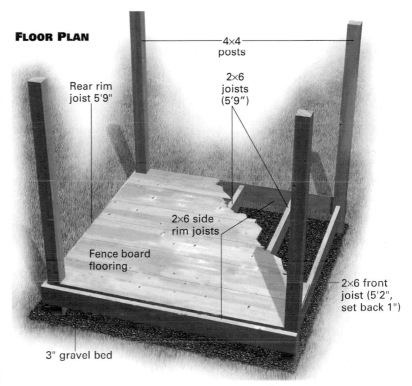

**FLOOR PLAN**

4×4 posts

2×6 joists (5'9")

Rear rim joist 5'9"

2×6 side rim joists

Fence board flooring

2×6 front joist (5'2", set back 1")

3" gravel bed

## SETTING THE GRAVEL BASE

The gravel base will have a natural tendency to creep over time, but you can minimize the creeping by installing forms. Clear an area about an inch deep—slightly larger than the site—and dig narrow trenches 4 inches deep along the perimeter. Nail 2×4 stakes to 2×8 forms and drive the forms into the trenches, leaving about 3 inches above grade. Lay landscape fabric inside the forms to prevent weeds from growing. Pour and tamp the gravel and spread some on the outside of the forms if you don't want them to show. A cubic yard of gravel will cover about 80 square feet on a 3-inch base.

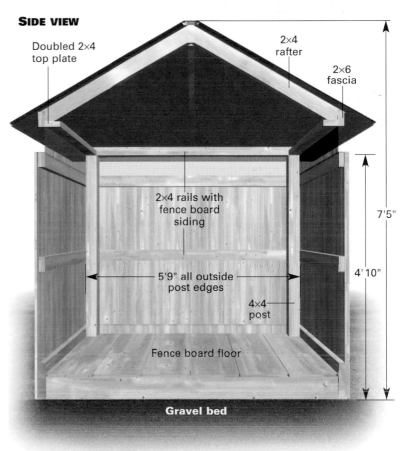

**SIDE VIEW**

Doubled 2×4 top plate

2×4 rafter

2×6 fascia

2×4 rails with fence board siding

5'9" all outside post edges

4×4 post

Fence board floor

Gravel bed

7'5"

4'10"

# LOW-SLUNG STOWAWAY
*continued*

**ROOF FRAMING**

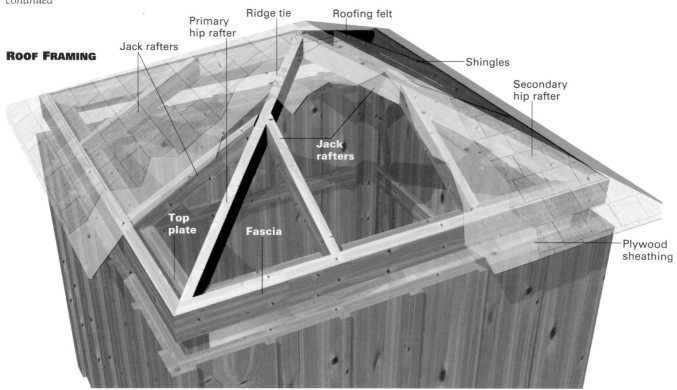

Labels: Ridge tie · Primary hip rafter · Jack rafters · Roofing felt · Shingles · Secondary hip rafter · Jack rafters · Top plate · Fascia · Plywood sheathing

**RAFTER DESIGN**

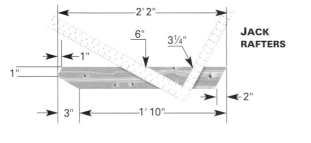

JACK RAFTERS
2' 2" · 6" · 3¼" · 1" · 1" · 3" · 1' 10" · 2"

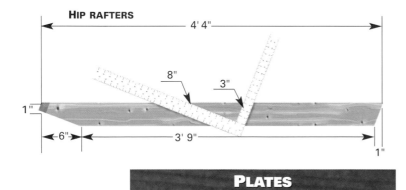

HIP RAFTERS
4' 4" · 8" · 3" · 1" · 6" · 3' 9" · 1"

## PLATES

Mark one of the posts at 5 feet, 8 inches above the bottom of a rim joist and use a water level to mark the other posts. Cut all the posts to this length.

Cut (at 5 feet, 9 inches) and miter the doubled 2×4 top plates. Nail the first one flat to the top of the posts and the second to the first. Tie the corners together with angle brackets. Then cut at 6 feet, miter the 2×6 fascia, and nail it to the top plates flush at the bottom.

## RAILS

Cut the rails the same length as the rim joists and nail them to the posts. Mount the upper rail 10 inches below the top plate and the lower one midway to the floor.

## ROOF

Carefully mark and cut the rafters for the roof framing according to the rafter diagram at *left*. Note that the bottom ends of the rafters fit into the ledge formed by the fascia where it meets the top plate (*see illustration above*).

■ Mark the rafter angles, using a carpenter's square. The primary and secondary rafters are beveled and angled at the bottom ends to fit snugly in the mitered fascia corners. Note that the primary hip rafters are ¾-inch longer than the secondary hip rafters. The jack rafters are angled and squared at the bottom to fit against the fascia, and beveled at the top to fit against the hip rafters. Note these top bevels are cut one way for "right-handed" jack rafters and the other way for their "left-handed" counterparts.

■ To assemble the framing, set the primary hip rafters in place, and toenail the top ends together with two 8d nails. Then toenail the bottom ends to the plates with two 16d nails.

■ Install the secondary hip rafters in the same way. Finally, nail the jack rafters to the hip rafters with two 8d nails at the top and at the bottom with two 16d nails.

■ Cover the roof framing with rough-sawn fencing or exterior-grade plywood. Run sheathing about halfway up the roof and trim it in place. Use the cutoffs to finish up to the peak. Tie the edges with ridge ties. Complete the roof with 30-pound felt and composition shingles.

## SIDING

Side the shed with fence boards or exterior-grade plywood. Hide the joints between the boards with 1×2 battens, and complete the corners with 1×4 trim. Cover the space between the siding and the top plates with hardware cloth to keep insects out.

## GATES

Measure the height you want for the gates (in this design, about 4 feet 10 inches) and the width, about ½ to ¾ inch narrower overall than the opening. Build them of siding boards nailed to a Z-shape 2×4 frame (*similar to the door-building process, described on page 53*). Place the bottom rails high enough to clear the floor when the doors are installed. Attach T-hinges, then hang the doors by fastening the hinges to the front posts. Finish the installation with a latch or slide bolt and with a stop nailed to the top plate to keep the gates from swinging too far inward.

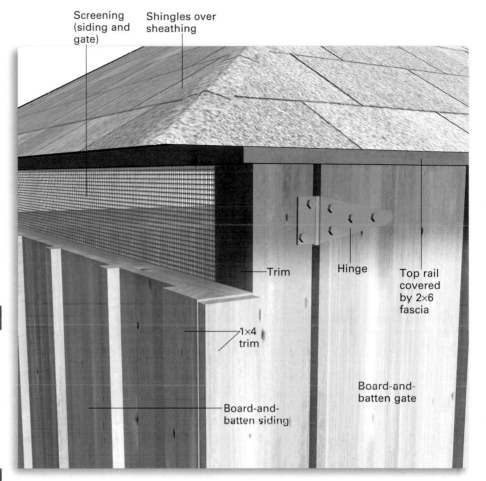

Screening (siding and gate)

Shingles over sheathing

Trim

Hinge

Top rail covered by 2×6 fascia

1×4 trim

Board-and-batten siding

Board-and-batten gate

## TAKE IT EASY

If you plan to store heavy or bulky lawn equipment, such as a large mower, consider adding a ramp to ease the task of getting it out and putting it away. The ramp design on page 49 can be easily adapted for most needs.

## MATERIALS FOR LOW-SLUNG STOWAWAY

| Description | Material | Size | Quantity |
|---|---|---|---|
| Post footings | Concrete | 60 lb. concrete mix | 8 |
| | Gravel | | ½ cu. yd. |
| Lumber | Posts | 4×4, 10' minimum | 4 |
| | Floor joists | 2×6 lumber, 6' | 7 |
| | Top plates, rails, rafters, gates | 2×4 lumber, 6' | 27 |
| | Fascia | 2×6 lumber, 6' | 4 |
| | Floor sheathing, roof sheathing, siding | 1×12 rough sawn fence, 6' | 18 |
| | | 1×12 rough sawn fence, 8' | 24 |
| | Trim | 1×2 battens, 5' | 20 |
| | | 1×4 corner, 5' | 8 |
| Roofing | Comp. shingles or type you choose | | 67 sq. ft. |
| Hardware | Gate hinges, latches, cane bolt | | as required |
| | Screen | ⅛ hardware cloth | 12 sq. ft. |
| | Nails | 16d sinker | 5 lb. |
| | | 8d HDG | 5 lb. |
| | | Roofing as required | |

# VERSATILE GARDEN TENDER

With a slightly oriental flavor, this structure combines plenty of storage with relaxed work space for gardening, picnicking, or just taking a break. A locked storage room protects equipment, tools, and chemicals. The design will easily accept a concrete, stone, or brick-surfaced entryway.

## SQUARING THE BEAMS

Despite your best efforts, a beam or two may sometimes wander slightly out of plumb. Here's how to bring the errant members to their rightful places: Loop a length of rope around the beams just under the beam location. Tie the rope in the center and use a 2×4 to twist it. Pull the beams in place and have a helper fasten the beams to the posts.

## POSTS AND FOUNDATION

Using the illustration *opposite*, lay out the site with batter boards and mason's lines. For more information on layout procedures, see *page 10*. Dig postholes 3 to 4 feet deep and 12 to 18 inches wide, and pour in 4 inches of gravel. Set and plumb the posts (use decay-resistant or pressure-treated wood), brace them, and pour the concrete.

Using the dimensions on the illustration *opposite*, set up batter boards and mark the outline for the concrete slab foundation. In this design, the storage room and shelving structure—including the doorway entrance—sit on a concrete slab, but you also can lay out the whole site for a slab or other surface if you want. For a slab, excavate to a depth of 8 inches—for 4 inches of gravel and 4 inches of concrete—and build 2×8 forms staked every 24 inches. Pour the gravel base and concrete.

When the concrete is still wet, set J-bolts every 2 feet and let the concrete cure for three days to a week. (see *pages 11* and *39* for more information about slab construction.)

## POSTS AND BEAMS

Mark one corner post at 7 feet, 5½ inches from the ground and cut it at the mark. Using a carpenter's level and 2×4—or a water level—cut the other posts.
■ Using the techniques discussed on page 21, notch the corner and side beams (1½×5½ inches).
■ Miter the 4×6 beams and cut 1½-inch notches on the inside surfaces where they will meet the notched posts. When assembled, the outside edges of the beams should be flush with the outside edges of the posts.
■ Fasten the beams to the corner posts with ⅜×6-inch washered lag screws and to the side posts with ⅝×3½-inch carriage or hex-head bolts. Strengthen joints with corner brackets.

## FRAMING

As with most other structures, it's better to build the walls on the ground. Use pressure-treated lumber for the sill plates and be sure to mark and drill them for J-bolt anchors.
■ Using the diagram at *right*, measure and cut the sill and top plates. The doorway wall has a doubled top plate (not shown) that extends across the door opening to the stub wall. The top plate of the stub wall is also doubled.
■ Cut the studs at 6 feet, 9 inches and assemble each section (studs inside plates). Where a wall meets a post, it begins with a stud, and walls not nailed to posts terminate with doubled studs. When the sections are assembled, move them in place. Bolt the sill plates to the J-bolts and nail the frames to the posts and beams. Then build the door and windows with jack studs, cripple studs, and headers (*see page 46*).
■ If you plan to use board siding, toenail horizontal 2×4 rails at the top and middle of each frame to provide a nailing surface; rails are not necessary for plywood sheathing.

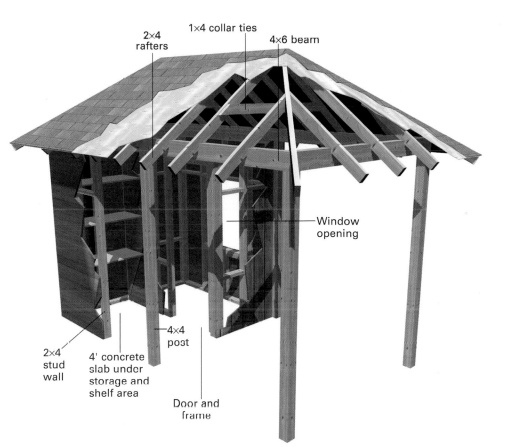

1×4 collar ties
2×4 rafters
4×6 beam
Window opening
4×4 post
2×4 stud wall
4' concrete slab under storage and shelf area
Door and frame

**WALL FRAMING**

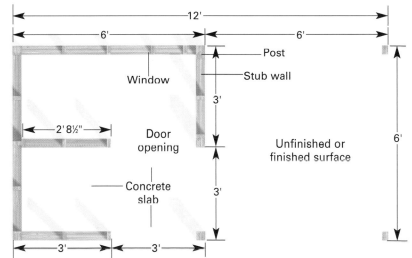

12'
6'
6'
Post
Window
Stub wall
3'
2' 8½"
Door opening
Unfinished or finished surface
6'
Concrete slab
3'
3'
3'

## SAFETY FIRST

Cutting posts requires you to work from a ladder or scaffold, so be careful, wear eye protection, and make sure the ladder or scaffold is stable.

# VERSATILE GARDEN TENDER
*continued*

## SIDING

Cover the exterior walls and sides of the shelf recess with board-and-batten siding, lap siding, or exterior-grade plywood. Create a tiny attic over the storage area with a ½-inch plywood ceiling supported by 2×4 joists. Now you're ready to build the roof structure.

## ROOF FRAMING

Four elements make up the roof framing:
■ **THE RIDGE BOARD:** a 2×6 forming the peak of the roof.
■ **COMMON RAFTERS:** 2×4s connecting the ridge to the beams.
■ **HIP RAFTERS:** 2×4s connecting the ridge to the corners.
■ **JACK RAFTERS:** 2×4s connecting the hip rafters to the beams.

Start with the easiest cut—the ridge board. Cut it to 6 feet, 2 inches and set it aside. Using the diagram below as a guide, cut each set of common, hip, and jack rafters and label them. Cut each rafter in this sequence.

**COMMON RAFTERS:** Cut the common rafters to the length shown. Then mark the angles with a carpenter's square. Note that the two end rafters are 1 inch shorter than the rest.

**HIP AND JACK RAFTERS:** These rafters have a compound miter at the upper end, and you will need an equal number of each that are "right handed" and "left handed." Follow these steps to cut them:
■ Mark the uncut rafter stock at the lower point of the compound miter.
■ Using a carpenter's square set at the measurements shown in the diagram, mark the angle of the miter.
■ Set your circular saw for a 45-degree bevel and cut half of the rafters at the angle line you marked. For the other half of the set, turn the rafter over and measure and cut as above.
■ Measure from the other end to the bottom of the beam notch, and using the same measurements on the framing square, mark and cut the notch.

## RAISE THE ROOF

You'll need two helpers for this step.
■ Mark the rafter locations on the beams and the ridge. Install rafter brackets on the beams at your marks.
■ With two helpers holding the ridge, nail one of the middle common rafters and then nail its opposite.
■ Nail the next middle pair. If you've cut the rafters to the measurements shown in this design, the top of the ridge should be 10 feet, ½ inch off the ground, give or take a little, due to slight variances in cutting angles.

Install the remaining middle rafters.
■ The common rafters on the end are last. Nail them so their top edge is ⅝ inch below the top of the ridge (to accommodate the roof sheathing).
■ Measure, cut, and nail collar ties to link the end pair of middle rafters so the walls won't spread under the roof's weight.
■ Now you can attach the hip rafters and then the jack rafters with two 16d nails in each end. Check the angles on the hip and jack rafters to make sure the cuts fit correctly; they won't fit right if you try to use the wrong one.

**ADJUSTMENTS:** Ideally, everything should fit plumb, level, and flush. There is always something, however, that conspires to make misfits of one or more rafters. Make minor adjustments by shaving a little off the end of a rafter or opening up the beam notch. But don't make any adjustments larger than ½ inch; if you're this far off, something's wrong and you need to recheck your measurements, angles, and cuts.

**RAFTER DIAGRAM**

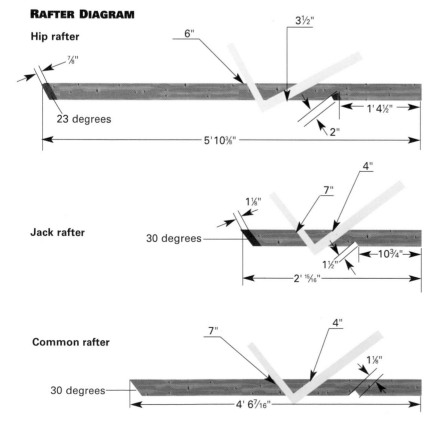

Hip rafter

⅞"
23 degrees
6"
3½"
1' 4½"
2"
5'10⅜"

Jack rafter

1⅛"
30 degrees
7"
4"
1½"
10¾"
2' 15⁄16"

Common rafter

7"
4"
1⅛"
30 degrees
4' 6⁷⁄16"

## ADDING ELECTRICITY AND WATER

Adding electricity and water will turn your shed into a useful workroom for gardening and other hobbies.

Lights and electrical outlets for power tools make an outdoor workroom even more useful. Turning on a nearby faucet is easier than dragging a heavy garden hose to water the plants, and a utility sink makes cleanup easy.

Most local codes require permits for this kind of project, so check first with your building department.

Even if your local code does not require that electric wires be buried, that is the tidiest and safest option. Wires should be enclosed within waterproof metal conduit. Water lines must be installed in the ground, below the reach of the worst winter's freeze.

Wiring and plumbing are beyond the scope of this book, but the work itself is not especially difficult. Wiring and plumbing involve methodical, step-by-step procedures that you will find outlined in specialized instruction books.

## ROOF FRAMING

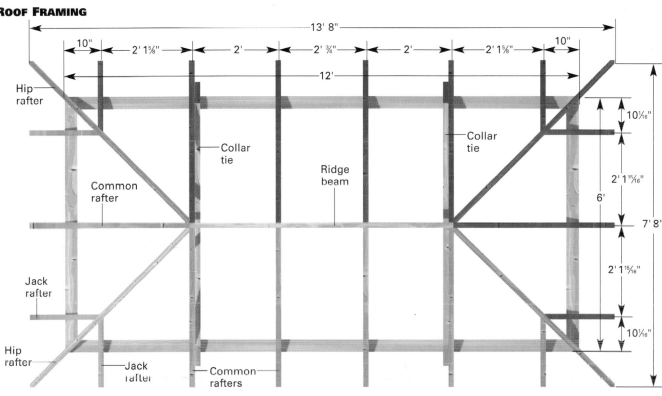

# VERSATILE GARDEN TENDER
*continued*

## ROOF

With all the rafters in place, cover the roof with ⅝-inch plywood or 1×6 boards. Install plywood sheathing (make sure it's exterior-grade stock) in full sheets, and trim the edge of each slope in place with a circular saw. Save the pieces you cut off; you can use them on another side.

To protect the sheathing, improve waterproofing, and provide a consistent surface for attaching shingles, apply 30-pound roofing felt over the sheathing. Use the fasteners recommended by the manufacturer (usually staples applied with a staple hammer) available at your rental outlet. The cost is nominal, considering the time you'll save.

Install whatever roofing material you prefer. Choose material that matches or complements your yard, garden, landscape, or other structures on your property.

## FINISH WORK

Complete your storage shed by installing the window, door, and shelving in the recess and inside the storage room.

■ **PRE-HUNG WINDOWS:** You can find myriad choices available in several stock sizes; check with your lumber yard or building center. You shouldn't have trouble finding one to fit the opening in this design.

Some pre-hung windows are unfinished and others are primed but not painted, letting you choose the stain or paint that best matches your design. Still others come prefinished and are ready to install.

■ **DOORS:** Check building supply centers for a door that complements your design. You can cut down the top of a standard-sized solid core door to fit the 24×74-inch opening specified in this plan.

■ **POTTING BENCH:** This structure can be easily adapted by adding a potting bench along the open back wall. Provide for additional storage for pots and gardening supplies underneath. A handy water supply and electrical outlets complete the gardening center.

*The storage area of this garden tender is just the size to handle a variety of light-duty garden and hand tools—as well as the variety of stuff that tends to accumulate during outdoor projects. Take advantage of the wall space and hang perforated board to keep the clutter to a minimum. Use the attic shelf to store things you don't use often. Remember space-saving hooks and hangers.*

## STORAGE DEVICES AND HARDWARE

Storage gadgets jam the aisles of home supply and building centers. Every year they add some miracle invention to help you live a tidier life. Here are some tried and true favorites:

■ **PERFORATED BOARD:** Brackets and hooks keep things in sight and close at hand on a wall of perforated board. Look for hangers that snap into the perforations.

■ **BICYCLE HOOKS:** Screw them into rafters to hang heavy stuff overhead, clearing valuable floor space. Many threaded hooks have thick shanks, so drill pilot holes to prevent splitting wood.

■ **SHELF BRACKETS:** Several types of ready-made brackets hold shelves for paint cans, tools, and other small items. Tip: They inevitably get overloaded, so make sure the brackets and shelves have more support than you expect will be needed.

■ **HOSE RACK OR REEL:** A tangle of hose can make a mess of your new shed. Tame those hoses with brackets made just for this purpose. You can make your own or go shopping; either way, make sure you drain hoses well before storing them for the winter.

## MATERIALS FOR GARDEN TENDER

| Description | | Material/Size | Quantity |
|---|---|---|---|
| Foundation | Storage slab and post footings | Concrete | ½ cu. yd. |
| Framing | Posts | 4×4 lumber*, 10' minimum | 6 |
| | Beams | 4×6 lumber, 12' | 3 |
| | Sill plates | 2×4 lumber, (PT) 12' | 3 |
| | Walls: top plates, studs, rails | 2×4 lumber, 8' | 36 |
| | Ceiling framing | 2×4 lumber, 10' | 3 |
| | Rafters | 2×4 lumber, 10' | 10 |
| | Ridge | 2×6 lumber, 8' | 1 |
| | Collar ties | 1×4 lumber, 12' | 2 |
| | Roof sheathing | ⅝" exterior plywood, 4×8 sheets, or | 8 |
| | | 1×6 boards | 310 lin. ft. |
| | Miscellaneous scrap for bracing | | |
| Roofing | | 30-lb. roofing felt | 167 sq. ft. |
| | | Shingles | 167 lin. ft. |
| Siding | | 1×12 lumber rough sawn, 8' | 22 |
| Trim | | 1×2 battens, 8' | 14 |
| | | 1×3 corner trim, 8' | 12 |
| Door | | 24"×74" pre-hung or cut from solid core | 1 |
| Window | | 18"×36" | 1 |
| Shelving | | 2×8 lumber, 8' | 4 |
| Hardware | Post-to-Beam bolts | ⅜×6 lag screws | 16 |
| | | ⅜×3½ machine bolt | 4 |
| | Nails | 16d sinker | 5 lb. |
| | | 8d sinker | 5 lb. |
| | | 8d HDG | 3 lb. |
| | J-bolts | ⁷⁄₁₆×6 | 10 |

*Redwood, cedar, cypress, or pressure treated*

## VERSATILE GARDEN TENDER
*continued*

### ADD A SUNNY DISPOSITION TO THE GARDEN TENDER

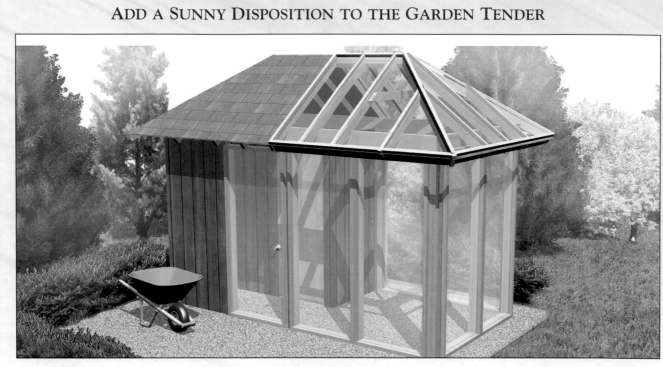

You can adapt this structure to create a combined storage shed and warming house by covering part of the roof with acrylic sheets. Acrylic lets sunlight and heat in and keeps warm air from leaving, providing a cozy, humid atmosphere for starting new plants and flowers. Use the acrylic to enclose the sides, too, and make an acrylic door set in a 2×4 frame. Because of the air space above the beam, you won't get a full "greenhouse" effect, but the air inside will be substantially warmer and more humid than in an uncovered structure.

Glazing comes in a range of sizes, thicknesses, and colors. Use clear acrylic if you live in a temperate area. If the location of the structure gets intense sun, consider using tinted acrylic, which reduces heat and glare. Climate also affects the thickness of glazing you should choose. Select $3/16$-inch stock unless your area regularly receives winter snow; for such areas, choose $1/4$-inch (or thicker) sheets.

Acrylic glazing comes from the factory with a protective paper or plastic film. Don't remove it until just before you are ready to install each sheet. The film guards against scratches and scuffs during handling, cutting, and drilling. Once you've installed the glazing, you can easily peel it off.

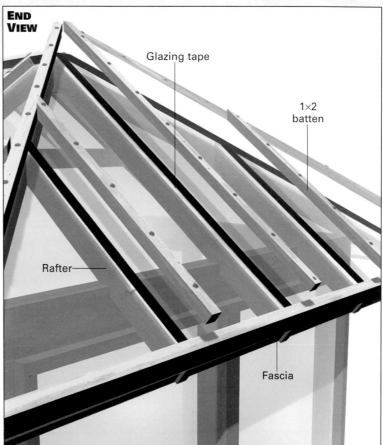

END VIEW

Glazing tape

1×2 batten

Rafter

Fascia

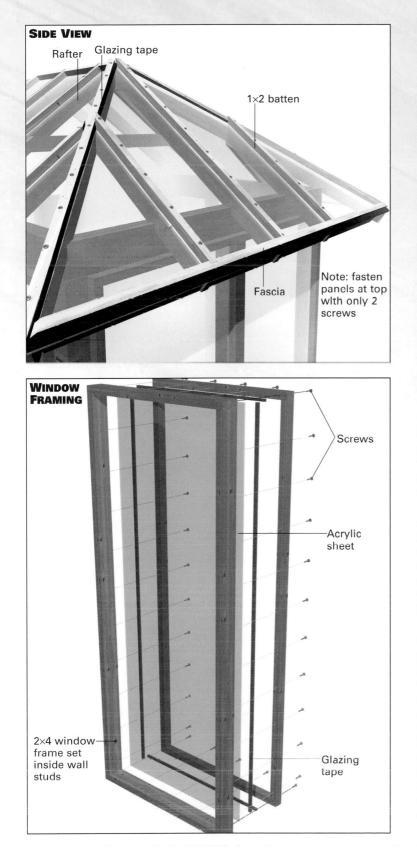

**SIDE VIEW**

Rafter
Glazing tape
1×2 batten
Fascia
Note: fasten panels at top with only 2 screws

**WINDOW FRAMING**

Screws
Acrylic sheet
2×4 window frame set inside wall studs
Glazing tape

■ **MODIFICATIONS:** To adapt the design for use as a greenhouse, complete the roof framing as described in the directions for the garden storage shed *(see pages 60-61)*. Cover the storage and shelving areas with plywood sheathing or 1×6s as described in the previous plan, but leave the remaining framing uncovered. Skirt the rafter ends with a 2×4 or 2×6.

Finish the solid roof by covering the plywood sheathing with roofing felt and shingles. Then cover the remaining portion of the roof with $3/16$- to $1/4$-inch (or thicker) acrylic sheets, cutting them $1/4$ inch shorter than the rafter ends to let the rain run off.

■ **EXPANSION ROOM:** Fasten each acrylic panel to the framing with at least two galvanized wallboard screws spaced no more than one foot apart. Leave a $1/4$-inch gap between adjacent panels to allow for expansion due to temperature changes. (With an 80° F variation in temperature in a year—not unusual in many areas— a 4-foot wide acrylic panel will expand more than $1/4$ inch).

Seal all joints with glazing tape $1/2$ inch wide by $1/4$ inch thick. Glazing tape is a heavy, self adhesive caulk with a peel-off paper cover on one side. You'll find it at your local glass supplier. It is easier and much less messy than using caulk from a tube and caulking gun.

Run a strip of glazing tape along the top and bottom of each panel and along both sides. Peel off the paper cover. Press a strip of sheet metal flashing into the glazing tape along the tops of the panels at the roof ridge, and along the hip rafter joints. Fasten the flashing in place with sheet metal screws. Finally, cover the joints at the rafters with 1×2 battens fastened with screws attached to the rafters in the space between adjoining panels.

■ **ADDING WINDOWS:** To add side windows, build 2×4 frames on the ground and attach them to the posts and beams with screws. Install acrylic panels in the frames, working in a similar fashion as on the roof. Frame a door in the same way. When summer days sizzle and it's just too warm for the side walls, you can remove them easily: Simply take out the screws and store them so the plastic glazing doesn't get scratched or scuffed.

# PLAYMATE: THE SHED WITH A DUTY TO HAVE FUN

## ROUND THE EDGES

Use a router and a roundover bit, a block plane, or a rasp and sandpaper to smooth the edges of the posts, ladder rails, door and window openings—any surface that may produce splinters.

## FULL COVERAGE

You can leave this playhouse to weather in the elements, but it will be more attractive if you stain or paint the wood. Use only high-quality, nontoxic, heavy-duty, chip-resistant finishes.

## LOCAL CODES

Before beginning any construction project, check your local building codes for any special requirements that may affect your plans. Some local codes will require footings instead of concrete-filled postholes.

Children seldom need help to spark their imaginations—but when they do, this playhouse comes packed with versatility. The lower room turns into a puppet theater or a grocery store. The second floor becomes a stage, the deck of a ship, or the terrace of a mansion overlooking the sea. There's a firehouse pole for a quick getaway and a sandbox to make the landing soft.

Although the playhouse construction may look somewhat complicated, it actually goes together rather simply—one step at a time.

## POSTS

Your posts should be pressure-treated (rated for ground contact) or a naturally resistant species, such as redwood, cypress, or cedar.

The five posts that form the downstairs room extend through the deck to support the second story guardrail. Two of the other posts extend to only the height of the deck and a third (at the ladder opening) is mounted to a joist below the deck surface.

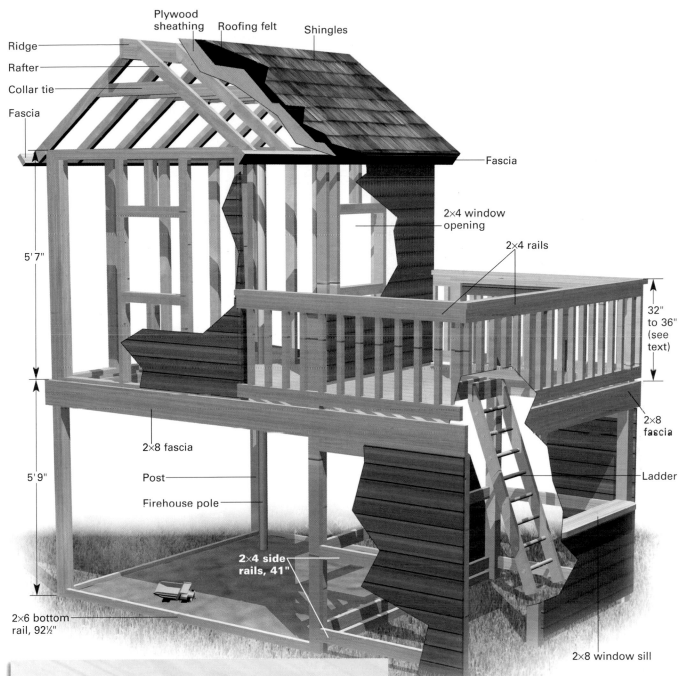

Ridge
Rafter
Collar tie
Fascia
Plywood sheathing
Roofing felt
Shingles
Fascia
2×4 window opening
2×4 rails
32" to 36" (see text)
2×8 fascia
Ladder
2×8 fascia
5' 7"
2×8 window sill
2×8 fascia
Post
Firehouse pole
5' 9"
2×4 side rails, 41"
2×6 bottom rail, 92½"

## CHILDREN LOVE TO GARDEN

Since children love to dig in the dirt, encourage them to plant a garden alongside the playhouse. Easy-to-grow flowers include snapdragons, marigolds, nasturtiums, and zinnias. Remember vegetables, such as peas, cherry tomatoes, lettuce, herbs, or pumpkins and squash.

Use the layout plan on *page 68* and mark the centers of the postholes with batter boards and mason's lines (*see page 10*). Dig 4-foot postholes 12 to 18 inches wide; pour in 4 inches of gravel. Plumb and brace the posts and fill the holes with concrete. When it's cured, cut the posts— the short rear posts at 5 feet, 9 inches, and those that extend above the deck at 8 feet, 1½ inches.

## SANDBOX

This plan calls for a sandbox on the lower level below the firehouse pole. Make sure the 2×8s around the perimeter of the sandbox are pressure treated. Sink the boards so that the top edges are about 3 inches above the ground. Excavate the area inside the perimeter to a depth of at least 6 to 8 inches and fill it with good, clean sand, such as washed plaster sand from concrete or masonry supply outlets.

# PLAYMATE: THE SHED WITH A DUTY TO HAVE FUN
*continued*

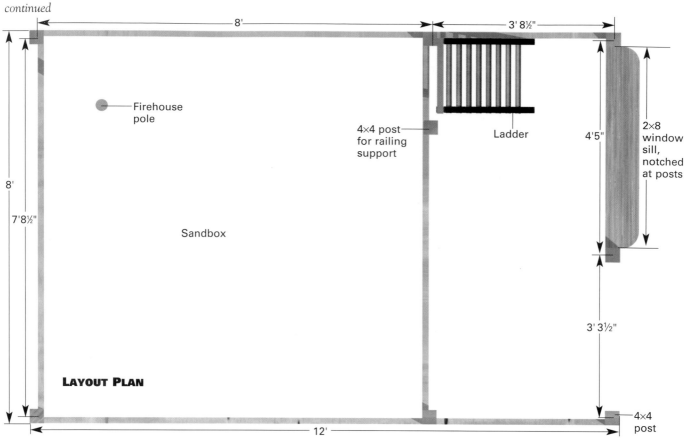

Firehouse pole

4×4 post for railing support

Ladder

2×8 window sill, notched at posts

8'

7'8½"

Sandbox

4'5"

3' 8½"

3' 3½"

**LAYOUT PLAN**

12'

4×4 post

## RUBBER CHIPS

Rubber chips made from recycled tires—available in some areas—are a good alternative to sand, wood chips, and other cushioning materials in play areas. Check with parks or school administrators to locate a supplier. Whatever material you choose, use plenty of depth to soften those inevitable falls.

## DECK

Mark the posts at 5 feet, 1¾ inches above the ground and then install the 2×8 fascia that's attached to the exterior of the posts.

■ Cut the fascia to length (8 feet on the ends and 12 feet on the long sides) and fasten it to the outside face of the posts at the marks. Use two ⅜×4-inch lag screws at each post (offset on the sides of the corner posts so they don't run into each other).

■ Working inside the framework, measure between the posts and cut 2×6s to fit inside each section. Fasten them to the posts with angle brackets flush with the bottom of the 2×8s. This leaves a ledge around the edge, which supports the ends of the flooring. Drive two 10d nails every foot through the 2×8s.

■ Fasten joist hangers to the 2×6s on 24-inch centers and nail the floor joists in the hangers. Note that the center wall of the roofed section is supported

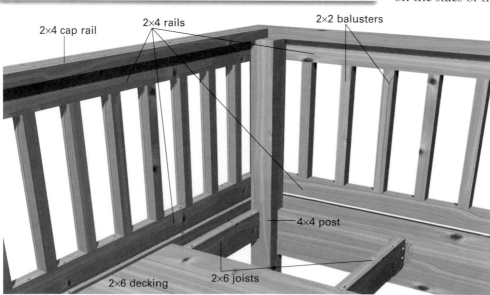

2×4 cap rail

2×4 rails

2×2 balusters

4×4 post

2×6 decking

2×6 joists

by a double 2×6 joist—use a hanger made for doubled 2×6s.

■ Use the framing plan on page 69 to cut the remainder of the framing pieces and attach them with joist hangers. Then bolt the short post to the joists, using two ⅜×6-inch countersunk bolts in each direction.

■ Measure and cut the 2×6 decking and nail it to the joists, snug against the 2×8 rim joists.

## DOWNSTAIRS ROOM

To build the walls for the downstairs room, use the illustration on page 67 as a guide and measure, cut, and toenail 2×4 rails between the posts with 8d nails. Set the upper rail under the 2×6 joist, the lower rail 1 to 3 inches above ground, and the middle rail at mid-point. Then apply the plywood siding, using 6d HDG nails every 6 inches. Make the front window sill from a 2×8, notched at the back corners so it will fit around the posts, and attach it to the posts and the 2×4 middle rail with 16d finish nails. Round the front corners with a router.

## UPSTAIRS ROOM

The upstairs room is built with conventional 2×4 stud-wall framing.

■ To begin, cut the top and bottom plates for the front and back walls (see the plan, *above*).

**UPPER LEVEL PLAN**

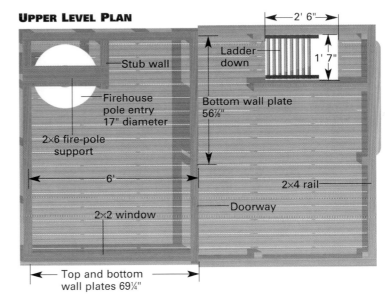

Then cut the 2×4 studs to 64-inch lengths. Mark the plates for stud locations (24 inches on center), then assemble the framing, with two 16d nails driven through the plates into each stud. Erect the frame and nail it to the deck, bracing it with 2×4s.

■ Measure for plates, and erect the rest of the framing in the same manner, allowing for window and door openings—build these after bracing the walls. Then frame the short stub

**DECK FRAMING PLAN**

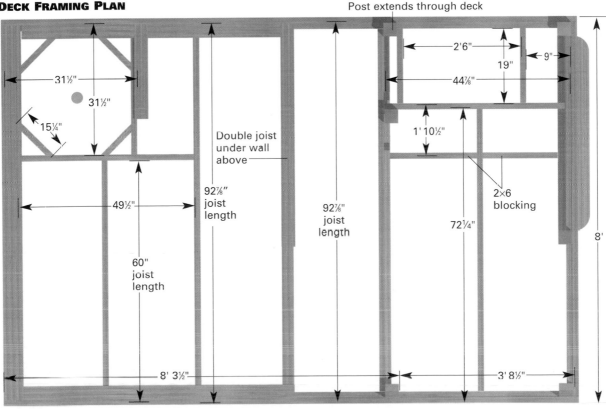

# PLAYMATE: THE SHED WITH A DUTY TO HAVE FUN
*continued*

## ROOFING PLAN

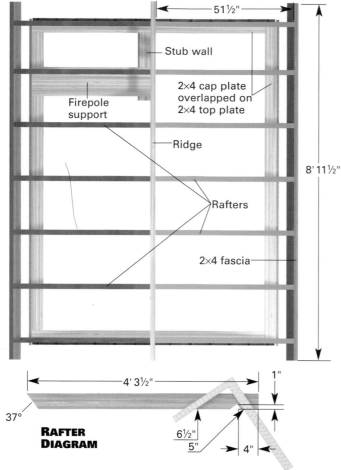

- Stub wall
- 2×4 cap plate overlapped on 2×4 top plate
- Firepole support
- Ridge
- Rafters
- 2×4 fascia

51½"

8' 11½"

4' 3½"

1"

37°

6½"
5"
4"

**RAFTER DIAGRAM**

across the rafters. If you alter this design, make sure the collar ties are high enough so taller visitors won't bump their heads.

Cut and nail the 2×4 fascia to the ends of the rafters and cover the framing with ½-inch exterior-grade plywood. Finish by applying roll roofing or shingles over roofing felt.

## RAILING

Build the railing sections on the ground and install the assemblies or build them in place. The railings in our design are made of 2×2 balusters fastened between 2×4 rails set on edge, but you can design a different style railing. Whatever you choose, measure the post-to-post span (inside or outside dimensions) and cut 2×4 top and bottom rails to these lengths. Screw them to the exterior (or interior) of the posts. Then cut enough 2×2 balusters to fill the length of the railing. Space them less than 4 inches or more than 8 inches apart so that small children can't get their heads caught between them. Screw the balusters to the rails, and finish the railing with a 2×4 top rail mitered at the corners.

## LADDER

The ladder is made of two 6 foot, 2 inch 2×4s and eight 18¾-inch lengths of 1¼-inch dowel. Cut the tops and bottoms of the rails so the ladder stands at a comfortable angle for young climbers. Measure eight equally spaced marks

wall that partially encloses the firehouse pole. It consists of a top and bottom plate (length of your choice) and two studs.

■ Tie the walls (including the stub wall) together with a 2×4 cap plate nailed to the top plate. The cap plates cross the corners to tie one wall to the adjoining one. Install the 2×6 firehouse pole support by nailing it to the cap plates of the outside and stub walls.

■ Install the plywood siding as you did on the lower room.

## ROOF

To frame the roof, cut seven pairs of 2×4 rafters and the ridge board to length (see roofing and rafter plan, *above*). With a helper holding the ridge, toenail a pair of rafters at one end of the ridge and to the cap plates (with three 8d nails at each end). Then do the same at the other end of the ridge. Cut seven 1×4 collar ties to 30-inch lengths and angled to match the rafter angle. Nail them

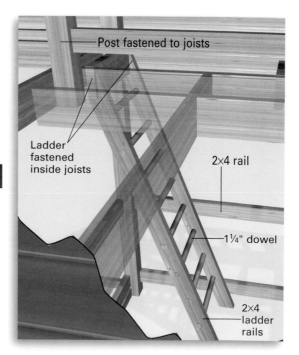

- Post fastened to joists
- Ladder fastened inside joists
- 2×4 rail
- 1¼" dowel
- 2×4 ladder rails

on one of the ladder rails, then clamp it to the other and drill 1¼-inch holes through both pieces. Drive the dowels through the holes with a mallet (don't force them or you might split the rails). Countersink 3-inch screws through the edges of the rails into the dowels. Secure the ladder to the joist at the edge of the opening with countersunk deck screws. Finish by mounting 24-inch grab bars to the railing posts on the deck on either side of the ladder opening.

## FINISHING TOUCHES

Make the firehouse pole out of a 12-foot length of 1½-inch galvanized pipe, secured with a pipe flange on the upper 2×6 support and set in concrete in a 1-foot-deep hole. Install and trim the windows. Use a router or sander to round off edges where little fingers might catch splinters. Then protect your work with a coat of paint or stain. For a super playhouse, finish the interior with sheet rock, carpeting, and kid-size furniture.

## MATERIALS FOR PLAYMATE

| Description | | Material/Size | Quantity |
|---|---|---|---|
| Framing | Posts | 4×4 lumber*, 10' | 3 |
| | | 4×4 lumber*, 14' | 5 |
| | Fascia joists | 2×8 lumber, 8' | 2 |
| | | 2×8 lumber, 12' | 2 |
| | Deck joists and blocking | 2×6 lumber, 8' | 13 |
| | Decking | 2×6 lumber, 12' | 17 |
| | Upper and lower rails | 2×4 lumber, 12' | 25 |
| | Rafters and fascia | 2×4 lumber, 10' | 9 |
| | Ridge | 2×6 lumber, 10' | 1 |
| | Roof sheathing | ½" plywood, 4×8 sheets | 3 |
| | Siding | T 111 plywood, 4×8 sheets | 9 |
| Roof | Roll roofing | 90-lb. | 1 roll |
| Miscellaneous | Firehouse pole | 1½" diameter galvanized pipe (threaded one end), 12' | 1 |
| | | 1½" pipe flange | 1 |
| | Window sill | 2×8 lumber, 6' | 1 |
| | Sandbox header | 2×6 lumber, 8' | 4 |
| | Sand | Washed plaster sand | 1½ cu. yd. |
| | Ladder rails | 2×4 lumber, 6' | 2 |
| | Ladder rungs | 1¼" dowels | 10 lin. ft. |
| | Grab bars | 24" | 2 |
| Railing | Rails | 2×4 lumber, 12' | 6 |
| | Pickets | 2×2 lumber | 160 lin. ft. |
| Hardware | Joist hangers | 2×6 | 9 |
| | | Doubled 2×6 | 1 |
| | Angle brackets | Standard | 12 |
| | Screws (railing and ladder) | 3" coated deck screw | 2 lbs. |
| | Bolts (short rail post) | ⅜×6" carriage bolt w/nut and washer | 4 |
| | Fascia joist screws | ⅜×4½" lag screw w/washer | 22 |
| | Nails | 16d sinker | 5 lb. |
| | | 8d sinker | 2 |
| | | 16d HDG | 6 |
| | | 10d HDG | 2 |
| | | 8d HDG | 5 |
| | | 1½" joist hanger nails | 1½ lb. |

*Redwood, cedar, cypress or pressure-treated

# STRUCTURAL BACKPACK

This utility shed attaches easily to the side of your house or garage and provides storage and quick access to garden tools and supplies. Its design offers an added benefit: You can build it as a freestanding structure if you don't have a wall that's convenient to attach it to. Just change the rear studs to 4×4 posts set in concrete, adjust the length of the side rails, roofing, and rafters, and add sheathing to the back.

Add a shelf or worktop, move the shed close to the garden and it's a potting shed for light- to medium-duty gardening chores. If you leave the shed unfinished, use naturally resistant woods. If painting best complements your outdoor design, use less expensive grades, and posts rated for ground contact.

## MARKING THE LOCATION

Attached to an existing structure, the shed requires two 2×6 ledgers—one for the roof and one for the floor. Locate the shed so the roof ledger is centered between the house wall studs—look for a nail line in the siding or use a stud finder to locate them. Mark the location of the roof ledger and drop a plumb bob to mark the position of the floor ledger.

## SETTING THE FLOOR LEDGER

Cut the floor ledger to length (see diagrams, opposite). Install it at least 3 inches above the ground to allow for air circulation and to avoid conditions that will cause rot.

**FLOOR DIAGRAM**

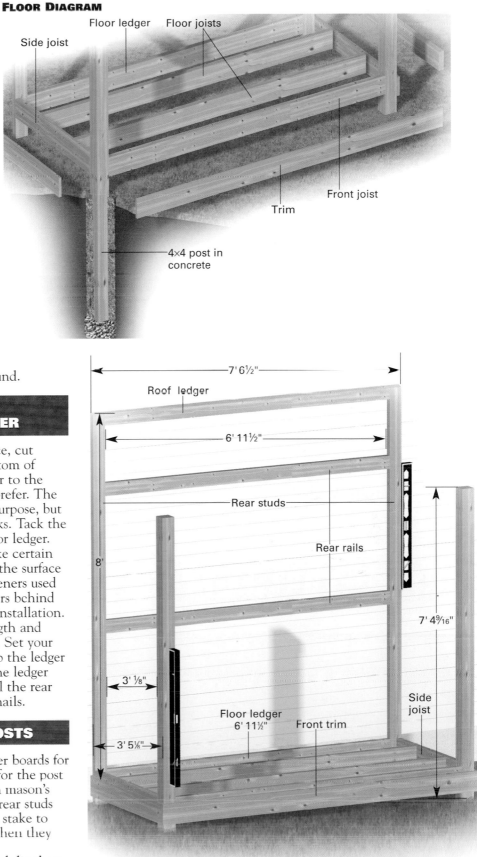

If you're attaching to a masonry wall, prop or tack the ledger temporarily in place and mark its location on the wall. Starting ¾ inch from the end, drill ½-inch holes counterbored for washers every 10 inches. Drive in masonry anchors and fasten the ledger, using ½×5-inch lag screws with washers.

If your house has clapboard siding, mark and drill as above, but add washers between the ledger and the siding to make the ledger perpendicular to the ground.

## REAR STUDS AND ROOF LEDGER

When the floor ledger is in place, cut the rear studs, either to the bottom of the ledger (8 feet, 5½ inches) or to the ground—whatever length you prefer. The extra length has no structural purpose, but you may like the the way it looks. Tack the rear studs to the ends of the floor ledger. Using a carpenter's level to make certain they are plumb, fasten them to the surface of the house with the same fasteners used for the floor ledger, using washers behind the studs as in the floor-ledger installation. Then cut the roof ledger to length and bevel its top edge at 20 degrees. Set your circular saw to the angle and rip the ledger along its length. Then attach the ledger with the same fasteners. Toenail the rear studs to both ledgers with 16d nails.

## FOOTINGS AND POSTS

If you don't want to set up batter boards for such a small project, set stakes for the post corners and square the site with mason's lines run from the edges of the rear studs and around the perimeter, from stake to stake. Measure the diagonals; when they are equal, your site is square.

Mark the posthole centers and dig them 4 feet deep. Check with your local building

# STRUCTURAL BACKPACK
*continued*

## FRAMING DIAGRAM

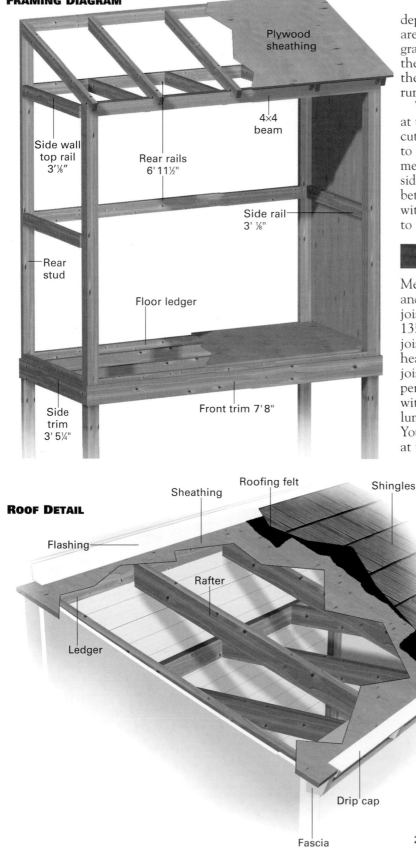

Plywood sheathing

4×4 beam

Side wall top rail 3'⅛"

Rear rails 6'11½"

Side rail 3'⅛"

Rear stud

Floor ledger

Side trim 3'5¼"

Front trim 7'8"

department to confirm the frost depth in your area before you dig footings. Pour 4 inches of gravel in each hole, set the posts—bracing them plumb—and pour the concrete. Slope the top edge of the concrete to allow rain to run off and let it cure for three to seven days.

When the concrete is cured, mark one post at the height shown (7 feet, 4⅝ inches) and cut it. Use a water level or carpenter's level to mark the other post and cut it also. Then measure between posts and studs and cut the side and front joists. Toenail the side joists between the posts and rear studs and flush with the outside faces. Toenail the front joist to the posts.

## JOISTS AND FLOORING

Measure the length between the side joists and cut the floor joists. Fasten evenly spaced joist hangers to the side joists (at about 13½ inches on center) and install the floor joists. If your flooring will have to support heavy loads, install evenly spaced joists in joist hangers (spaced about 11 inches apart) perpendicular to the ledger. Cover the floor with ¾-inch, exterior-grade plywood or 1×6 lumber, cut out for the posts at the corners. You may be tempted to install the 1×6 trim at this point, but wait until you've completed the side framing to make the siding fit easier.

## BUILDING THE FRAME

Cut the front rail and toenail it to the top of the posts. Next measure and cut the 2×4 ceiling joists, and the rear and side rails to length and toenail them in place. Note that the side rails are flush with the outside post faces to provide a nailing surface for the siding. The middle rear rail does not have a structural function but is added to provide a nailing surface for shelving supports or a plywood sheet which could be installed to protect against equipment damage.

## ROOF DETAIL

Sheathing

Roofing felt

Shingles

Flashing

Rafter

Ledger

Drip cap

Fascia

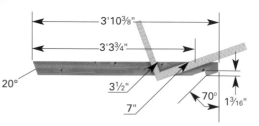

3'10⅜"

3'3¾"

3½"

20°

7"

70°

1³⁄₁₆"

## ROOF FRAME

To frame the roof, cut the five rafters, using the dimensions and angles shown in the rafter detail. Nail them between the beam and the rear frame members as shown in the illustration *below*. For greater strength, use rafter ties at the beam. Note that the end rafters are flush with the outside edges of the posts and beam.

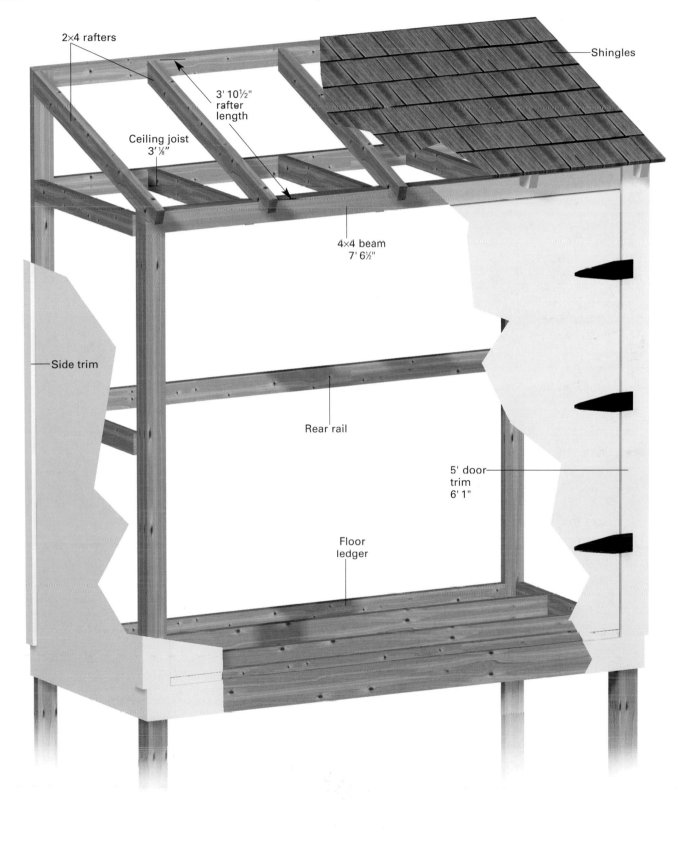

2×4 rafters

Shingles

3' 10½" rafter length

Ceiling joist 3' 1⅛"

4×4 beam 7' 6½"

Side trim

Rear rail

5' door trim 6' 1"

Floor ledger

# STRUCTURAL BACKPACK
*continued*

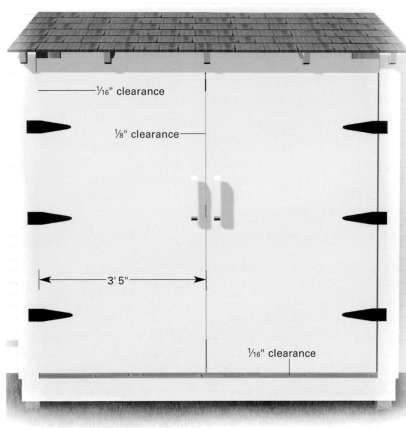

¹⁄₁₆" clearance

⅛" clearance

3' 5"

¹⁄₁₆" clearance

Use exterior-grade plywood siding or fence boards for the "skin" of your shed. Before installing the siding, measure 8 feet down from the top of the roof ledger and mark the side joists at that measurement. Nail the side 1×6 floor trim pieces at the mark. This will allow a full sheet of plywood to fit the sides.

■ **SIDE WALLS:** If you use plywood, hold up the sheet against the frame and mark its interior side where it meets the rafter and front post. Take the sheet down and cut it on your marks. If you use fencing, use the same method with each board, but start fence boards on the front post and rip the board closest to the house to fit the space remaining. Attach the

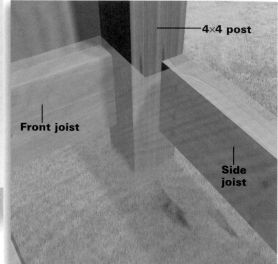

4×4 post

Front joist

Side joist

## MAKE THE MOST OF YOUR SHED SPACE

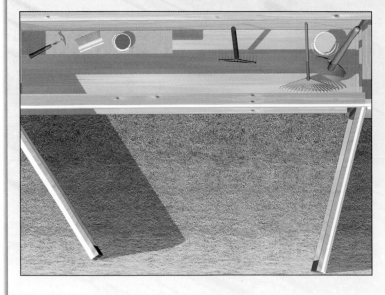

Once you've finished building the attached shed, it's easy to add shelves and a worktop to make the most of the space available. This illustration shows how you might use the shed for light gardening duties and to store yard supplies.

Choose your shelving material carefully. Here are some tips:
■ Solid wood is strong, comes in standard widths, and is easy to cut to length.
■ Plywood is both strong and stable, especially in thicknesses of ½ inch or greater.
■ Particleboard is heavy and cumbersome. Since it sags, give particleboard shelving short spans and plenty of support.

If you will use the shed to store lawn equipment, such as a mower, consider adding a ramp like the one shown on *page 49.*

siding to the framing with 8d nails. Then measure, cut, and install the 1×3 side trim.

■ **ROOF SHEATHING:** You won't need to cut the roof sheathing—the shed is designed to use a single sheet of ¾-inch exterior-grade plywood. Install the sheet flush with the outside edges of the structures and nail it to the rafters and the roof ledger, tight against the house surface.

■ **MAKING IT WATERTIGHT:** Clean the joint between the roof sheathing and the house wall and run a bead of siliconized caulk in the joint to make it watertight. Cover the plywood sheathing with roofing felt and shingles, and complete the installation with a metal drip cap along the bottom edge.

## DOORS

Construct the double doors by building a pair of simple 2×4 Z-frames covered with the same siding as the walls. Using the information for building a Z-frame door (*see page 53*), measure your door opening and cut the door framing members to length. Your overall doorway should allow ⅛ inch for expansion.

Rip the 5-inch front trim from a 1×6 and nail it in place. Hang the doors with strap or T-hinges, install a latch or slide bolt to hold the door shut, and nail a stop block to the top of the door frame to keep the door from swinging inward.

## FINISHING TOUCHES

Finish the attached shed by painting or staining it to match the house, garage, or other structure to which it is attached. Install brackets to the inside walls of the shed to hang garden tools and other equipment. Add a chipboard or plywood backing if you wish.

## MATERIALS FOR STRUCTURAL BACKPACK

| Description | Material | Size | Quantity |
|---|---|---|---|
| Post footings | Concrete | | 2 to 3 cu. ft. |
| Lumber | Posts | 4×4 lumber,*10' | 2 |
| | Rear studs | 2×4 lumber, 10' | 2 |
| | Roof ledger | 2×4 lumber, 8' | 1 |
| | Floor ledger and joists | 2×6 lumber, 8' | 5 |
| | Floor trim and fascia | 1×6 lumber, 8' | 2 |
| | Flooring | 1×6 lumber, 8' | 17 |
| | Rails and ceiling joists | 2×4 lumber, 8' | 7 |
| | Rafters | 2×4 lumber, 6' | 3 |
| | Door framing | 2×4 lumber, 8' | 3 |
| | Beam | 4×4 lumber, 8' | 1 |
| | Edge trim | 1×3 lumber, 8' | 4 |
| | Front trim | 1×6 lumber, 8' | 4 |
| Doors | Door frames | 2×4 lumber, 8' | 8 |
| | Door sheathing | ¾-in. exterior-grade plywood siding, 4×8 sheets | 2 |
| Roof | Sheathing | ¾-in. exterior-grade plywood 4×8 sheet | 1 |
| | Roofing | 30-lb. felt, composition shingles | 54 sq. ft. |
| Siding | | ¾-in. plywood siding 4×8 | 2 |
| Hardware | Assorted 16d nails and 3-in. decking screws | | |
| | Lag screws, ⅜×5, as needed for ledger and rear studs | | |
| | Assorted metal fasteners per text | | |

*Cedar, redwood, cypress, or pressure-treated

# GAZEBO BUILDER'S TRIO

*A gazebo is the structural equivalent of a hammock. It exists to soothe and comfort its occupants—allowing them to savor the breeze and the view and the fleeting time to enjoy them.*

*The classic and romantic gazebo is in high season during the long, sultry days and nights of summer. It also enhances fragrant spring mornings when trees have budded and flowers begin to bloom. And where would you rather enjoy a crisp autumn Sunday when brilliant leaves bejewel the yard? A gazebo beckons even in the sparkling snap of winter, when you find yourself watching crystalline breath as you gaze into the heavens atwinkle with starlight.*

*The gazebo can take many shapes, but the intent is always the same— to enjoy the beauty of a peaceful setting. The gazebos presented here include an elaborate design inspired by the Victorian age, a relaxed screened summerhouse, and a garden gazebo—a whimsical and updated version of this most classic of all outdoor structures.*

*As with other plans in this book, you can adapt these designs to suit your own location and preferences. You can build with confidence as long as you follow the recommendations that are given for footings and foundations, post heights, beam spans, and materials to handle the loads the structure will support.*

*The extra care you take in planning and building your gazebo will let you enjoy it that much more, and for that much longer.*

## SO WHAT IS A GAZEBO?

It's a fun word, one that puzzles linguists as well as do-it-yourself builders. Gazebo has Latin roots and refers to seeing a beautiful view. Certainly gazebos have captured their share of vistas, including shorelines, woodlands, and gardens. Architecturally, they're open shelters designed to command a view of nature. The heyday of gazebos stretched from the Victorian age through the roaring 1920s as people found the time and the means to enjoy their summers in leisure. Many public parks designed during this period featured a bandstand—which is just a larger version of the gazebo—for concerts performed by local musical groups, and for both down-home and national political oratory.

*This variation of the classic Victorian style gazebo adds a striking accent to the backyard landscape—yet its design and ornamentation is surprisingly easy to construct. Set on posts in concrete and with a raised floor, it offers a perfect spot for summertime family gatherings or solitary retreats.*

# VICTORIAN GAZEBO

**This octagonal plan is based on the classic Victorian gazebo, conjuring romantic images of peaceful contemplation, watching fireworks on the Fourth of July, or fireflies on an August evening.**

This elegant gazebo is built on a frame of 6×6 posts, 4×6 beams, and 2×6 rafters. The eight-panel roof is sheathed with 2×6 tongue-and-groove decking covered with roofing felt, and topped with composition or wood shingles.

Decorative touches include sturdy railings on seven of the eight sides, with latticework, graceful overhead arches, and a festive finial at the peak of the rooftop.

## SOME FOUNDATION FACTS

Your gazebo must be anchored securely to concrete footings, whether you build on a concrete slab, a brick patio, or a wooden deck. A poorly anchored gazebo can become a giant umbrella in a high wind, ready to fill with air and fly away. Use post anchors made for 6×6s; try to find one with 2¼-inch straps—the width of one of the post faces.

## LAYOUT

To establish the outline for the eight-cornered gazebo, measure out a 12-foot square. Set batter boards outside the corners and—using mason's lines—square it, using the "3–4–5 test." Here's how:

■ From the intersecting lines, mark a spot 3 feet out on one line and 4 feet on the other. Now measure diagonally between the two marks—if your corner is square, the distance between the marks will be 5 feet. Adjust and retest until it's perfect at all corners. Then drop a plumb bob from the intersecting lines and mark the points with stakes. These stakes do not represent post locations; they are the reference points from which you will measure to plot the centers of the posts.

■ Using the plan view (*see page 82*), measure from the stakes to the post centers. Drop a plumb bob and stake these points to mark the centers of the footing holes.

■ Dig footing holes—12 to 18 inches wide and as deep as local codes require. Pour a 4-inch gravel base in each hole and then pour the concrete. Set post anchors while the concrete is still wet and make sure your anchors are centered.

■ Run lines from the center of the anchors and measure carefully from one to another (refer again to the plan view). A misplaced post will cause mischief throughout construction.

Whether you're building on a deck, slab, or existing patio, orient the anchors so the inside faces of adjoining posts are parallel.

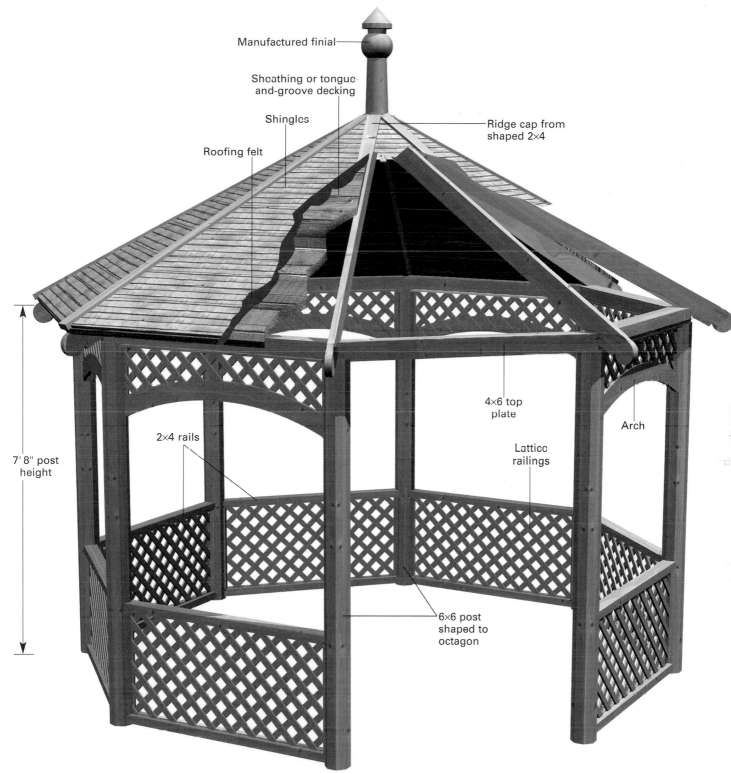

Manufactured finial

Sheathing or tongue-and-groove decking

Shingles

Roofing felt

Ridge cap from shaped 2×4

4×6 top plate

Arch

2×4 rails

Lattice railings

7' 8" post height

6×6 post shaped to octagon

## SHAPING AND SETTING POSTS

While the concrete is curing (three days to a week), make octagons of the 6×6 posts. Snap a chalk line along the length of the posts, 1⅛ inch from each corner. Set your circular saw at a 45-degree angle and rip the posts from end to end, using a rip guide and a new blade. If you bog down, make two shallow passes. Smooth away the saw cuts with a plane or belt sander (be careful with the belt sander; it whisks away a lot of wood quickly).

## WHICH WOOD?

Because gazebos are traditionally painted white, you can build this project with less expensive grades of wood, and the paint will cover any imperfections. If you want a gazebo with a stained or a weathered surface, use better grades of wood. Choose a suitable species, such as redwood, cedar, or cypress, which—though more expensive—will stand up to the elements better than untreated pine or fir.

## VICTORIAN GAZEBO

*continued*

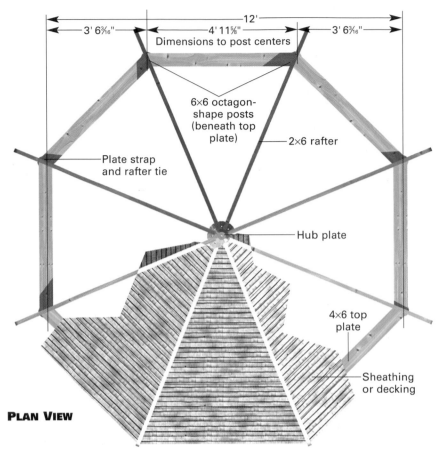

**PLAN VIEW**

Dimensions to post centers
12'
3' 6³⁄₁₆"    4' 11⁵⁄₈"    3' 6³⁄₁₆"

6×6 octagon-shape posts (beneath top plate)

2×6 rafter

Plate strap and rafter tie

Hub plate

4×6 top plate

Sheathing or decking

5 inches and the long side at 12 inches. Mark the angle on the 5-inch side. Make sure the angles are oriented the opposite way on each end of the top plates. Toenail the top plates to the posts with 16d hot-dipped, galvanized finish nails, and stiffen the joints with metal straps across the top of the plates.

■ Prepare for framing of the roof by nailing a rafter tie on the top plate, centered over each post. Make sure the structure is square and plumb before proceeding.

### ROOF FRAMING

The design for this gazebo calls for 2×6 rafters and a manufactured hub plate that ties them together at the peak. You also can make a wooden hub from a 6×6, using the same technique as you used for shaping the posts.

If you use a homemade hub, install 3×6 rafters, because a 2×6 is much narrower than the faces of the 6×6 octagonal hub. The 2½-inch thickness of a 2×3 is just slightly wider than the face of a shaped 6×6 hub, so if you use 3×6 stock, you will have to shave a bit from the ends to get them to fit the hub faces exactly.

The rafter and roofing configurations will also change, so you may have to experiment to get everything to come out right.

You can special-order 3×6 lumber if your supplier doesn't stock it.

The following instructions refer to a rafter installation using 2×6 stock.

■ When the concrete has cured and the posts are shaped, mark one post at 7 feet, 8 inches. Transfer the measurement to all eight sides of the post and use a circular saw to cut around it. Because the saw won't cut the full thickness of the post, finish the cut with a hand saw. Then install it in its anchor and brace it plumb on two sides with 1×4s staked in the ground.

■ Install and brace the next post and use a water level to mark its height. Take it down, cut it, and reinstall it. Repeat the procedure on the remaining posts.

■ You may consider using a helper (instead of braces) to hold the posts while you mark them. If you do so, make sure the posts are cut at the same length and are cut squarely.

■ Don't measure each post separately from the ground up. One anchor may be at a slightly different elevation, and even slight discrepancies in post heights will frustrate the rest of your efforts.

### INSTALLING TOP PLATES

■ Next, cut the top plates to length and miter each end at a 22½-degree angle. Mark the short side of your framing square at

### A GAZEBO WITH A HEX

Four-sided structures are easier to build than others. There's simply less geometry involved in building square corners. But an octagonal gazebo is easier to build than a hexagonal one. You can adapt this design to a hexagon by drawing a 5½-inch square on graph paper, measuring 60-degree angles from the center point and marking off six equal sides for cutting lines. Aside from the differences in angle and different measurements, the construction order for building a six-sided gazebo is the same.

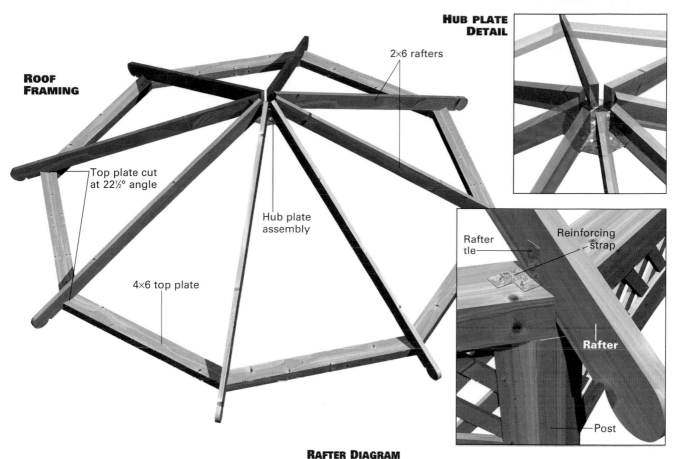

**HUB PLATE DETAIL**

**ROOF FRAMING**

2×6 rafters

Top plate cut at 22½° angle

Hub plate assembly

4×6 top plate

Rafter tle

Reinforcing strap

**Rafter**

Post

■ First mark and cut one rafter as shown in the illustration (*see above right*), mitering the peak end and using a saber saw to cut the eave end in a graceful arc or other decorative shape. Use this rafter as a template to cut the remaining seven.

■ Assembling the roof frame will require an assistant and scaffolding; you'll be working almost 12 feet up, so it's better to rent scaffolding sections.

■ Predrill holes in the peak ends of the rafters for the bolts used to fasten them to the hub plate. (Use the bolt sizes recommended by the manufacturer.) Hoist all eight of the rafters to the scaffolding, along with the hub plate.

■ Bolt the peak ends of two opposing rafters to the hub plate and swing the assembly into position.

**RAFTER DIAGRAM**

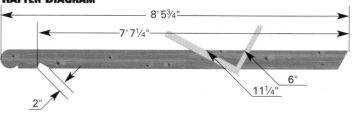

8' 5¾"

7' 7¼"

2"

11¼"

6"

**TOP PLATE DIAGRAM**

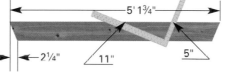

5' 1¾"

2¼"

11"

5"

## ROOF SAFETY

Assembling the roof framing is not difficult with an assistant, but it can be dangerous. Take care as you work: Watch where you stand and don't overreach when it would only take a moment longer to move a step closer.

## MAKING OTHER SHAPES

Gazebos are available in more shapes than octagons. There are other configurations and other manufactured hub plates to meet your designs. Hub plates like the one used in this design are available in 5-, 6-, and 8-sided models. Most building centers either stock such pieces or will order one. Mount a decorative finial on the hub to complete the gazebo peak.

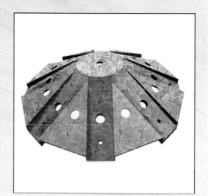

# VICTORIAN GAZEBO
*continued*

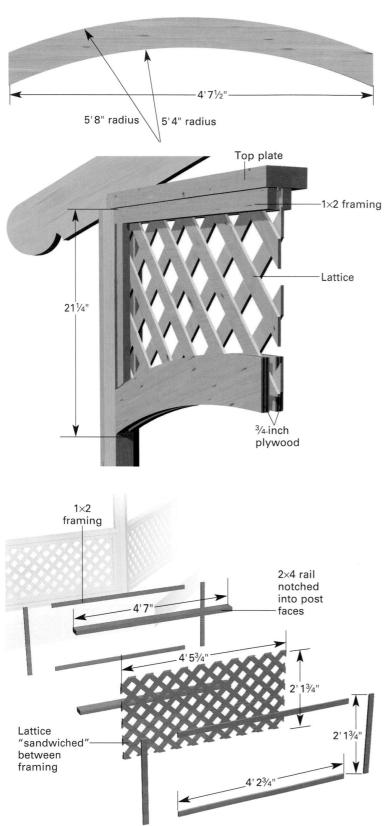

4' 7½"

5' 8" radius    5' 4" radius

Top plate

1×2 framing

Lattice

21¼"

¾-inch plywood

1×2 framing

2×4 rail notched into post faces

4' 7"

4' 5¾"

2' 1¾"

2' 1¾"

Lattice "sandwiched" between framing

4' 2¾"

■ With an assistant supporting the assembly at the hub, fit the eave ends of each rafter in the rafter ties and use 10d nails to secure them in place. As an assistant holds the hub and rafter assembly in place, install the remaining three pairs of opposing rafters. Then, top the hub with a decorative finial.

■ To install the tongue-and-groove decking, miter one end of each piece (4⅛ and 12 inches on the framing square) with your circular saw set at a 15-degree bevel. Install three or four boards at a time with two 10d nails at each end and trim off the excess (with the saw at the same bevel). Work from the bottom up and tack 2×4 cleats to the surface as you go.

Installing plywood sheathing will be a little more complicated. There will be more waste, and you might want to nail supports where the sheathing panels meet in each roof section. Lay one sheet lengthwise across the bottom of the rafters. Have your helper scribe the rafter lines—carefully—from underneath. Take the sheet down, mark a line ¾ inch inside the scribed lines, cut on that line, and nail it in place with the edges centered on the rafter.

■ Using this same procedure, work your way up the roof and install the remaining sheathing panels.

## ROOFING

When the decking or sheathing is in place, cover it with roofing felt, then shingles. Cover the hips with a ridge cap shaped from a 2×4, or use hip-and-ridge shingles.

## ARCHES AND LATTICE

Cut the pieces for the arches from ¾-inch plywood. Each arch requires two sides, and two plywood sheets will make all 14 pieces.

■ To mark and cut the first piece, center a nail on the plywood at the long radius (*see illustration top left*); scribe both lines. Cut one arch; use it as a template to cut the others.

## SITTING PRETTY

To appoint your gazebo in style, choose a table and chairs in a traditional, old-fashioned style—perhaps a few antiques purchased at a country auction or found in a second-hand store. Modern reproductions are easy to find. Metal furniture is best, painted white or shiny black. Avoid outdoor furniture made of lightweight materials such as aluminum or plastic, which can easily blow around in a storm.

■ Next, cut 1×2 framing pieces to length.

■ Using prefabricated lattice, measure and cut eight pieces to fit between the posts. Using an arch as a template, mark the lattice and cut it to the contour of the arch with a saber saw.

■ Screw all the pieces of the arches together with 2¼-inch screws and install the lattice and frame assembly between the posts, flush with the edges of the post faces. Nail or screw the 1×2 frame to the top rail.

■ Predrill the ends of the arch at a 45-degree angle and fasten the arch to the posts with 4-inch screws.

## RAILINGS

To construct the railings, cut 1½×⅝-inch notches in the posts (see page 84) and toenail the top and bottom rails in the notches. Then measure between the post faces and make sandwiched lattice panels as shown in the illustration. Install the lattice-panel assemblies by nailing or screwing the 1×2 frames to the posts.

## FINISHING TOUCHES

When the framing and finish work are complete, caulk or putty over any open joints, sand rough spots, and putty all nail and screw heads, driving the screws below the surface with an extra turn of your cordless drill and setting the finish nails with a nail set. Then seal or stain the structure or cover all exposed wood surfaces with a coat of good primer and two coats of enamel paint.

## MATERIALS FOR VICTORIAN GAZEBO

| Description | | Material/Size | Quantity |
|---|---|---|---|
| Foundation | Footings | Concrete | 1 cu. yd. |
| | Post base | 6×6 or column bases | 8 |
| Framing | Posts (longer lengths for use with raised deck | 6×6 lumber, 10' | 8 |
| | Hub (substitute for metal plate hub) | 6×6 lumber, 19" | 1 |
| | Top plates | 4×6 lumber, 12' | 4 |
| | Rafters | 2×6 lumber, 10' (optional 3×6s with wooden hub) | 8 |
| | Roof sheathing | ⅝-in. exterior-grade plywood | 16 sheets |
| | | (or 2×6 tongue-and-groove decking with 3×6 rafters) | (380 lin. ft.) |
| | Finial | Manufactured or homemade, 5" | 1 |
| Arches | Plywood | ¾" plywood, 4×8 sheets | 2 |
| | Latticework infill | | 80 sq. ft. |
| | Lattice framing | 1×2 lumber | 130 lin. ft. |
| Railings | Lattice framing | 1×2 lumber | 230 lin. ft. |
| | Lattice infill | | 115 sq. ft. |
| | Top and bottom rails | 2×4 lumber, 6' | 16 |
| Roofing | Underlayment | 30-lb. roofing felt | 1 roll |
| | Roofing | Shingles, type as chosen | |
| | Ridge caps | 2×4 lumber, 8' shaped | 8 |
| Hardware | Hub plate | Manufactured for octagon | 1 |
| | Post anchor bolts | As required | |
| | Plate strap | 12" | 8 |
| | Rafter ties | | 8 |
| | Screws | 2" drywall screw | 2 lb. |
| | | 4" drywall screw | 1½ lb. |
| | Nails | 10d box or sinker | 10 lb. |
| | | 16d HDG finish | 2 lb. |
| | | 6d HDG finish | 2 lb. |
| | Other hardware as required | | |

# SCREENED SUMMERHOUSE

*The design of this summer house was developed to cope with the insect problem inherent in many parts of the world. Screen panels are removable for repairs and off-season storage.*

With its wide eaves and raised cupola, this screened summer house is a shady, airy, and insect-proof retreat for picnicking, reading, or those rollicking family get-togethers.

## FOUNDATION

This summerhouse is shown on a concrete slab, but it could be built on a wooden deck, as long as the deck has adequate support to bear the weight of the walls. As with all outdoor structures, check with your local building department to make sure your plans meet all code requirements.

If you choose to build your gazebo or other outdoor structure over a wood deck, consider extending the deck beyond the perimeter of the summerhouse so you'll have plenty of room outside as well.

## POWER LOUNGING

Electricity will enhance the enjoyment of this summer house, adding the potential for reading lights so you can enjoy a good book on a quiet evening, a ceiling fan to provide a cooling breeze on a sultry summer day, or a television to follow your favorite sports team. Furnish the space for comfy lounging, which sets its own style.

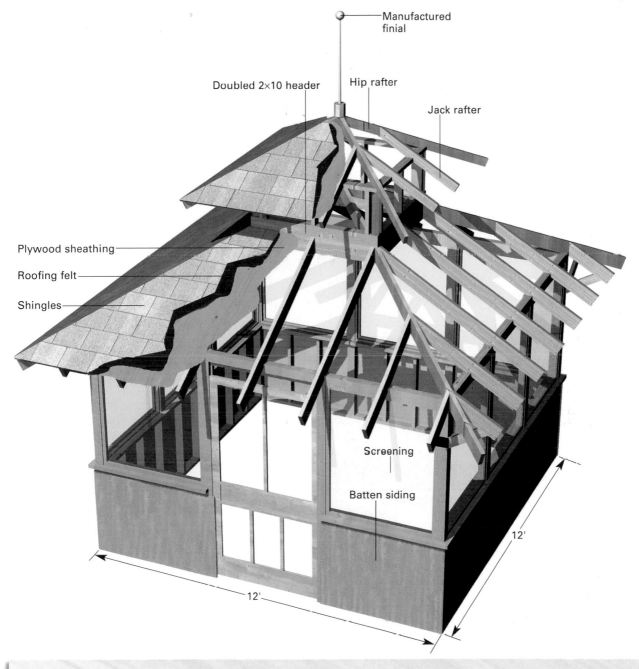

Manufactured finial

Doubled 2×10 header

Hip rafter

Jack rafter

Plywood sheathing

Roofing felt

Shingles

Screening

Batten siding

12'

12'

## SCREEN PANELS

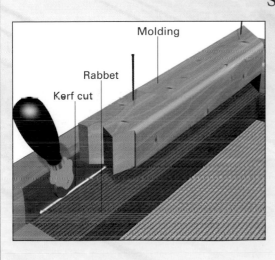

Molding

Rabbet

Kerf cut

To build the screen panels, make a rabbet cut along one side of 1×½-inch stock and cut a ⅛-inch kerf in the corner of the rabbet. Cut mitered framed pieces to length and screw and glue the corners to make a frame. Measure each opening separately—they're likely to vary slightly. Using lightweight, flexible fiberglass screen, cut pieces an inch or so larger than the frame opening to allow for overlap. After stapling the screen to the rabbet at the corners, use a screen splining tool—available at most hardware stores and building centers—to press the screen and a strip of vinyl spline into the saw cut. Trim off the excess screen and tack screen molding to hold it in place. Finish the job by installing the screen panels with 3-inch deck screws through the frame into the post. Replacing a damaged screen is easy—just remove the panel, repeat the process as described, and replace the panel.

## SCREENED SUMMERHOUSE
*continued*

### WALL FRAMING

If you're pouring a new slab, refer to pages 10 and 39 for slab-construction procedures, installing anchor bolts as required. If you're working with an existing slab, drill holes in the concrete for anchor bolts. If you are building this structure on a deck, you will screw the sill plates directly to the decking.

■ **FIRE UP THE POWER SAW:** Cut the pressure-treated sill plates for the walls to length. Also cut the twelve 4×4 posts to length (7 feet, 10½ inches), and notch the upper end of each for the beams (1½ inches × 3½ inches). See page 52 for notch-cutting techniques. Note that the corner posts are notched on two adjoining sides. Next, cut the 2×4 beams to length and miter the ends.

Temporarily place each sill plate in position and mark the locations for the anchor bolts, then drill holes for the bolts.

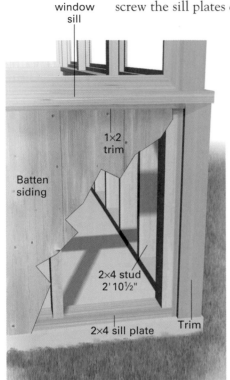

2×8 window sill

1×2 trim

Batten siding

2×4 stud 2'10½"

2×4 sill plate    Trim

**WINDOW DETAIL**

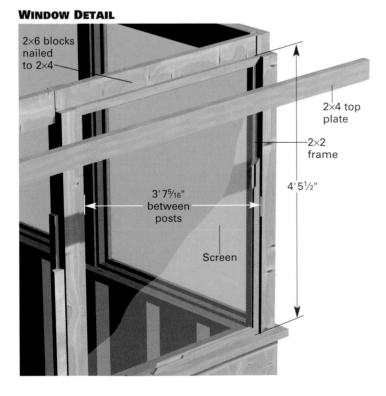

2×6 blocks nailed to 2×4

2×4 top plate

2×2 frame

3'7⁵⁄₁₆" between posts

4'5½"

Screen

Clamp each sill plate to its corresponding beam (with the sill plate flush at the inside of the miter) and mark the locations of the wall posts (4 feet on center from each end of the sill and 4 feet on center between the middle posts). These marks will help you to avoid inaccuracies later.

■ **START AT GROUND LEVEL:** Using the slab as a work surface, assemble one of the side walls first. Nail the sill plate to the posts with three 16d heat-dipped, galvanized (HDG) nails at each post. Then nail the beams into the notches in the top of the posts, using two 16d HDG nails for each post. Take care that the corners of the posts are snug inside the mitered beam. Finally, frame the lower sections of the wall—first toenail the 2×4 top rail to the 4×4 posts (3 feet from the bottom of the sill to the rail top), then nail the studs between the sill and the top rail on 16-inch centers.

■ **AN UPRISING:** With the anchor holes set on the anchors, raise the wall—but not quite plumb; lean it back an inch or two so that it will not get in the way when you raise its neighbors. Brace the wall in place temporarily.

Build and install the remaining walls. Note that the back wall is set inside the side walls (so its sill—and those of the front wall—does not have posts attached). The middle pair of posts on the front and back walls are set 24 inches from the outside edge of the structure.

When you've raised and braced all four walls, remove the temporary bracing from two adjacent walls and, with a helper, stand them straight up. Fasten the corners together with 16d sinker nails and corner brackets. Install the nuts on the sill plate anchor bolts. (If you are building over a wood deck, fasten the sill plates to the decking with wood screws.)

Complete the framing by cutting and installing the 2×6 blocks between the posts and behind the beams (flush at the top). Toenail the blocks to the posts and facenail them to the 2×4 beam. The face of the 2×6 extends below the beam to provide a lip that you'll attach the screen panels to. Then measure, cut, and install the ⅝-inch plywood siding. The plywood will hold the framing erect after you remove the temporary bracing.

Mark rafter locations on the tops of the beam and blocking (on 24-inch centers), and install rafter ties.

### ROOF FRAMING

With its cupola, this summerhouse actually has two roofs, both of them with the hip rafters that extend all the way to their peaks.
■ Using the rafter diagram (*see opposite page*), begin by cutting all the rafters for both roofs.

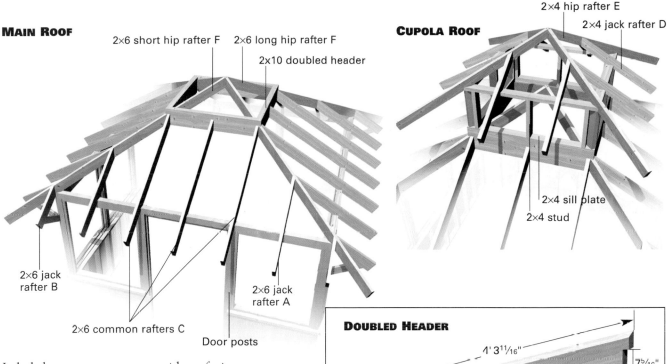

**MAIN ROOF**

2×6 short hip rafter F    2×6 long hip rafter F

2x10 doubled header

2×6 jack rafter B

2×6 common rafters C

Door posts

2×6 jack rafter A

**CUPOLA ROOF**

2×4 hip rafter E

2×4 jack rafter D

2×4 sill plate

2×4 stud

Label them as you cut to avoid confusion, and set the cupola rafters aside—you'll build it on the ground later.

■ Remember, you will need two sets for each length of jack rafter—one with left-handed miters and the other with right-handed miters. Follow these steps to cut them:

Mark the uncut rafter stock at the lower point of the compound miter. Using the measurements shown in the diagram, mark the angle of the miter. Set your circular saw for a 45-degree bevel and cut half of the rafters at the angle line you marked. For the other half of the set, turn the rafter over and measure and cut as above. Measure from the other end to the bottom of the beam notch. Using the same measurements on the framing square, mark and cut the notch.

Two of the hip rafters for each of the roofs will be ¾ inch shorter than the others— a length which allows them to meet the other hip rafters and still come out even on the bottom.

■ When you have the rafters cut, erect a section of rented scaffold and, with the help of an assistant, hoist the four hip rafters to the scaffold.

■ Attach the peak ends of the two long hip rafters, and swing the assembly into place. With your assistant supporting the joint, anchor the rafters to the rafter ties. Toenail the remaining two hip rafters to the first pair—at the peak and at the beam.

■ Mark the hip rafters for the doubled header. Cut the header pieces to length, then miter and notch them as shown in the illustrations *above*. Note that the headers are notched so they fit above the tops of the hip rafters. The inside surface of the notch is cut

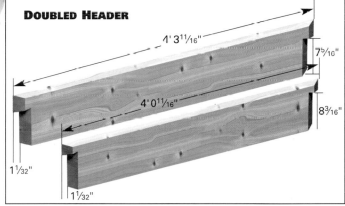

**DOUBLED HEADER**

4' 3$\frac{11}{16}$"

7$\frac{5}{16}$"

4' 0$\frac{11}{16}$"

8$\frac{3}{16}$"

1$\frac{1}{32}$"

1$\frac{1}{32}$"

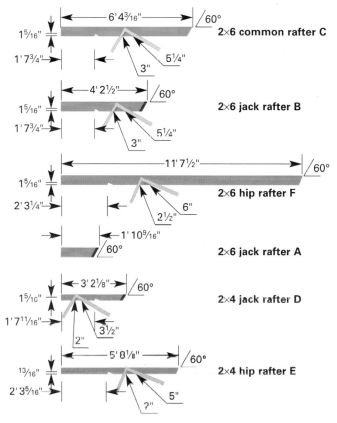

**RAFTER DIAGRAM**

6' 4$\frac{3}{16}$"    60°

1$\frac{5}{16}$"

1' 7$\frac{3}{4}$"    5$\frac{1}{4}$"    **2×6 common rafter C**

3"

4' 2$\frac{1}{2}$"    60°

1$\frac{5}{16}$"

1' 7$\frac{3}{4}$"    5$\frac{1}{4}$"    **2×6 jack rafter B**

3"

11' 7$\frac{1}{2}$"    60°

1$\frac{5}{16}$"

2' 3$\frac{1}{4}$"    6"    **2×6 hip rafter F**

2$\frac{1}{2}$"

1' 10$\frac{9}{16}$"

60°    **2×6 jack rafter A**

3' 2$\frac{1}{8}$"    60°

1$\frac{5}{10}$"

1' 7$\frac{11}{16}$"    3$\frac{1}{2}$"    **2×4 jack rafter D**

2"

5' 8$\frac{1}{8}$"    60°

$\frac{13}{16}$"

2' 3$\frac{5}{16}$"    5"    **2×4 hip rafter E**

?"

# SCREENED SUMMERHOUSE
*continued*

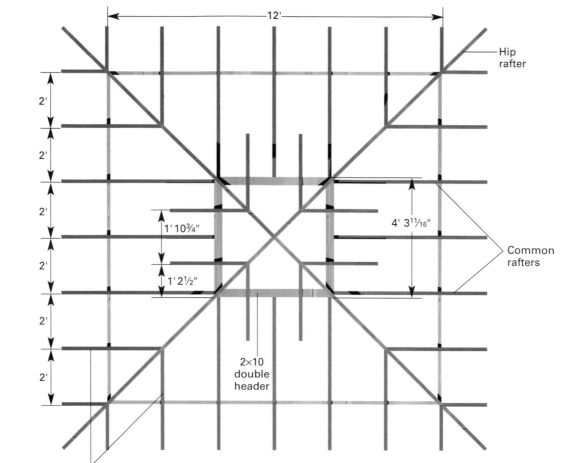

**ROOF FRAMING**

12'

Hip rafter

Common rafters

1' 10¾"

4' 3¹¹⁄₁₆"

1' 2½"

2×10 double header

2'
2'
2'
2'
2'
2'
2'

Jack rafter

## WINDOWSILL DIAGRAM

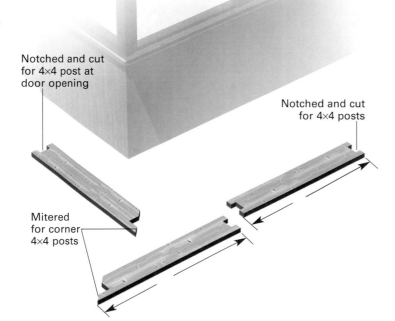

Notched and cut for 4×4 post at door opening

Notched and cut for 4×4 posts

Mitered for corner 4×4 posts

at a 45-degree angle, and bottom of the tab that extends over the hip rafters is mitered at a 60-degree angle.

Miter the full length of each header piece, then miter the bottom of the tab—just to the corner of the notch. Then miter the 45-degree cut for the notch and finish the cuts with a hand saw.

Nail the interior header to the hip rafters and then the exterior header. Fasten the header pieces to each other and screw the mitered corners to keep them from spreading. Once installed, the doubled header forms a flat surface for the cupola sill plate.

■ Toenail the common rafters to the doubled header. Then install the jack rafters as shown and measure, cut, and toenail the jack rafter supports to the posts.

■ Cut and nail the ⅝-inch plywood roof sheathing in place, centering joints over the rafters and working up from the bottom of the roof. Use plywood clips between the sections at horizontal joints. Nail 2×4 cleats along the way for footholds as you build. Now, you're ready for the cupola.

## MATERIALS FOR SCREENED SUMMERHOUSE

| Description | | Material/Size | Quantity |
|---|---|---|---|
| Framing | Posts | 4×4 lumber, 8' | 12 |
| | Sill plates | 2×4 lumber, 12' | 4 |
| | Beams | 2×4 lumber, 12' | 4 |
| | Blocks | 2×6 lumber, 12' | 4 |
| | Main roof rafters | 2×6 lumber, 12' | 180 lin. ft. |
| | Short walls; cupola hip, common, and jack rafters; blocking, braces | 2×4 lumber | 440 lin. ft. |
| | Rafter headers | 2×10 lumber, 10' | 4 |
| | Roof sheathing | ⅝ BCX plywood, 4×8 | 16 |
| Roofing | | 30-lb. roofing felt | 250 sq. ft. |
| | | Composition shingles | 250 sq. ft. |
| Siding and trim | Windowsills | 2×8 lumber, 12' | 4 |
| | Siding | ⅜ plywood siding, 4×8 | 6 |
| | Corner trim | 1×4 lumber, 8' | 4 |
| | Sill trim, door stops | 1×2 lumber, 12 | 280 lin. ft. |
| Screen panels | Frames | 2×2 lumber, 18' | 11 |
| | Screen | Fiberglass, 4' | 70 lin. ft. |
| | Trim | 1×1 lumber 18' | 11 |
| | Frame stop | 1×2 lumber, 18' | 11 |
| Hardware | Nails | 16d sinker | 10 lb. |
| | | 8d sinker | 5 lb. |
| | | 16d HDG | 2 lb. |
| | | 10d HDG | 2 lb. |
| | | 6d HDG | 4 lb. |
| | Mounting screws for screens | 3" deck screw | 2 lb. |
| | Assorted metal fasteners per text | | |

## BUILDING THE CUPOLA

While it will take some muscle and sweat to hoist the cupola into place, it's easier to build it on the ground as a complete unit, including the roof sheathing and the screening. Use the same techniques used for building the main roof to make the cupola. Nail the sill plate of the cupola to the doubled header.

Finish the two roofs by covering the sheathing on both the main and cupola roofs with roofing felt and shingles. If you use a corrugated metal roof, be sure to order metal hip caps and washered screws (the washers weal the screws from moisture).

## WINDOWSILLS, TRIM, AND SCREEN DOOR

With the framing for this summerhouse now complete, cut, notch (with a saber saw), and install the 2×8 windowsills. The sills cover the top exposed edges of the siding on the lower walls and provide a handy place for a tall, cool drink. Install the sills in sections.

Cut and install the 1×4 trim that covers the outside edges of the low wall siding, then the 1×2 trim under the windowsills.

Finally, cut and install the 1×2 screen stops to the posts and nail a 2×4 between the door posts at 6 feet, 8½ inches above the floor.

The door opening is designed for a 3-foot by 6-foot, 8-inch factory-built screen door. Remember to install a door-closer to prevent insects from swarming in through an open doorway.

## FINISHING TOUCHES

After installing the screen panels, finish the summerhouse. White, dark green, and black are traditional colors for such a structure, but you may choose any color, as long as it complements its environment. You also could stain the wood surfaces of this summerhouse and apply a clear finish.

# GARDEN GAZEBO

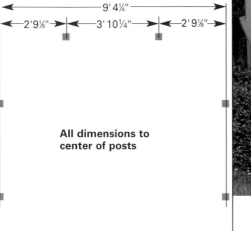

**PLAN VIEW**

9' 4¼"
2' 9⅛"   3' 10¼"   2' 9⅛"

All dimensions to center of posts

**BEAM LAYOUT**

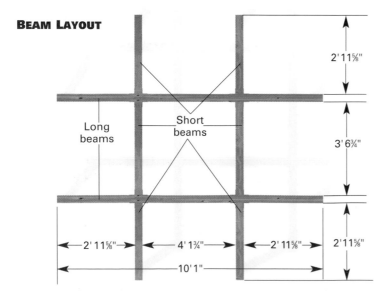

Long beams

Short beams

2' 11⅝"

3' 6¾"

2' 11⅝"

2' 11⅝"   4' 1¾"   2' 11⅝"

10' 1"

With its whimsical roof, this airy garden gazebo is perfect for a quiet corner to relax and enjoy the beauty of the garden.

The louvered roof will shed light rains and is tied together at the peak with a manufactured hub plate made for an octagonal gazebo. Such plates are available from your building-supply center.

## POSTS AND BEAMS

The posts for this garden gazebo can be anchored to poured concrete footings, a concrete slab, or nailed to the surface of a wood deck. The installation shown here is on a concrete slab.

Using the techniques for laying out the Victorian gazebo (*see page 80*), lay out the site, starting with a 9-foot, 4½-inch square. Refer to the plan view to measure the points for each post center, and mark them. Drill the slab for post anchors at these points (or stake for footings if you're starting from scratch). Attach the anchors.

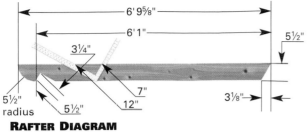

**RAFTER DIAGRAM**

■ Cut one post to length (7 feet), fasten it to its anchor, and brace it plumb. Hold the remaining posts in place and use a water level to mark them. Cut, install, and brace them.

■ Cut the long 4×4 beams to length (10 feet, 1 inch) and fasten them with post caps to opposing posts, making sure they overhang the posts equally.

■ Snap a perpendicular chalk line across the bottom of the long beams and mark the locations for the short-beam sections. Cut the short-beam sections to length; fasten them to the long beams with angle brackets and to the posts with post caps.

## ROOF FRAMING

Miter the 22½-degree angle on the 2×6 top-plate sections (use the 5- and 12-inch marks on a framing square) and attach them to the beams with 3½-inch galvanized screws. Strengthen the joint with angle brackets. "Cinch up" the mitered joints with two 3-inch decking screws. Install rafter ties on the top plate, centered on the joints.

■ Cut, miter, and notch the eight 2×6 rafters and predrill them for the hub plate bolts specified by the manufacturer. Starting 4⅞ inches from the top, mark the rafters every 10½ inches for the locations of the louvers. Erect a temporary scaffold (from your rental center) so you can complete the roof framing, and hoist the unassembled rafters to the scaffolding, along with the hub plate.

■ Attach an opposing pair of rafters to the hub plate; then, with an assistant, raise the paired assembly into position. Attach the rafters to the rafter ties at their notches.

■ Repeat the installation for the remaining rafters.

## LOUVERED ROOF

■ Miter the 2×10 louvers to the dimensions shown. Note that the cuts are compound miters. Mark the miter at 67 degrees using a framing square (use the 5 and 12 marks), and set your circular saw for a 6-degree bevel. Make the cuts. Install multipurpose angle brackets at the ends of each louver.

■ Working from the bottom, install each louver level at the marks on the rafters, bending the angle bracket to fit.

## GARDEN GAZEBO
*continued*

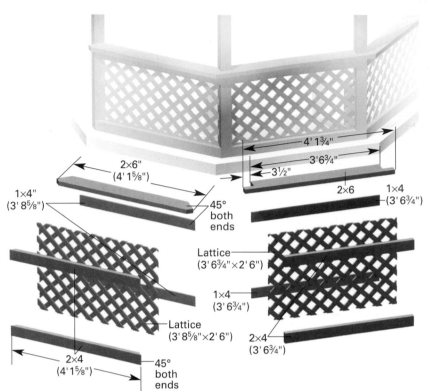

2×6" (4' 1⅝")

1×4" (3' 8⅝")

45° both ends

4' 1¾"

3' 6¾"

3½"

2×6

1×4 (3' 6¾")

Lattice (3' 6¾"×2' 6")

1×4 (3' 6¾")

Lattice (3' 8⅝"×2' 6")

2×4 (3' 6¾")

2×4 (4' 1⅝")

45° both ends

## RAILINGS AND BENCHES

Measure and cut the 1×4 and 2×4 side rail pieces as shown. Note that the lengths and angles alternate every other section. Assemble each section as a framed unit with lattice sandwiched between the frames and toenail the assemblies between the posts. Cut the 2×6 cap rail pieces and install them, too.

To complete construction of this garden gazebo, build the benches according to the dimensions shown. Assemble the 2×4 bench box supports with angle brackets and fasten them to the slab floor with anchor bolts.

## FINISHING TOUCHES

Finish this gazebo by painting all wood surfaces; it's easier to paint the individual pieces of the roof frame and louvered roof before assembling them. Or, use stain covered with a clear finish. Pots hung from the rafters and roof beams, filled with vines and flowers, complete the garden gazebo with a touch of the surrounding garden.

## MATERIALS FOR GARDEN GAZEBO

| Description | | Material/Size | Quantity |
|---|---|---|---|
| Framing | Posts | 4×4 lumber, 8' | 8 |
| | Beams | 4×4 lumber, 10' | 2 |
| | | 4×4 lumber, 12' | 2 |
| | Top plates | 2×6 lumber, 10' | 4 |
| Roof | Rafters | 2×4 lumber, 8' | 8 |
| | Louvers | 2×10 lumber, 8' | 13 |
| | | 2×4 lumber, 10' | 5 |
| Railings | Top rails | 1×4 lumber, 8' | 4 |
| | | 1×4 lumber, 10' | 4 |
| | Bottom rails | 1×4 lumber, 8' | 4 |
| | | 1×4 lumber, 10' | 4 |
| | Lattice | Manufactured lattice | 60 sq. ft. |
| | Cap rail | 2×6 lumber, 8' | 4 |
| | | 2×4 lumber, 10' | 4 |
| Benches | Seats | 2×6 lumber | 80 lin. ft. |
| | Bench box supports | 2×4 lumber | 40 lin. ft. |
| Hardware | Post anchors | | 8 |
| | Post/beam connectors | | 8 |
| | Multipurpose angle brackets | | 112 |
| | Angle brackets | | 36 |
| | Hub plate | | 1 |
| | Assorted fasteners according to text | | |

# INDEX

## METRIC CONVERSIONS

| U.S. Units to Metric Equivalents | | | Metric Units to U.S. Equivalents | | |
|---|---|---|---|---|---|
| To Convert From | Multiply By | To Get | To Convert From | Multiply By | To Get |
| Inches | 25.4 | Millimeters | Millimeters | 0.0394 | Inches |
| Inches | 2.54 | Centimeters | Centimeters | 0.3937 | Inches |
| Feet | 30.48 | Centimeters | Centimeters | 0.0328 | Feet |
| Feet | 0.3048 | Meters | Meters | 3.2808 | Feet |
| Yards | 0.9144 | Meters | Meters | 1.0936 | Yards |
| Square inches | 6.4516 | Square centimeters | Square centimeters | 0.1550 | Square inches |
| Square feet | 0.0929 | Square meters | Square meters | 10.764 | Square feet |
| Square yards | 0.8361 | Square meters | Square meters | 1.1960 | Square yards |
| Acres | 0.4047 | Hectares | Hectares | 2.4711 | Acres |
| Cubic inches | 16.387 | Cubic centimeters | Cubic centimeters | 0.0610 | Cubic inches |
| Cubic feet | 0.0283 | Cubic meters | Cubic meters | 35.315 | Cubic feet |
| Cubic feet | 28.316 | Liters | Liters | 0.0353 | Cubic feet |
| Cubic yards | 0.7646 | Cubic meters | Cubic meters | 1.308 | Cubic yards |
| Cubic yards | 764.55 | Liters | Liters | 0.0013 | Cubic yards |

To convert from degrees Fahrenheit (F) to degrees Celsius (C), first subtract 32, then multiply by $5/9$.

To convert from degrees Celsius to degrees Fahrenheit, multiply by $9/5$, then add 32.